TAL

MOSCOW

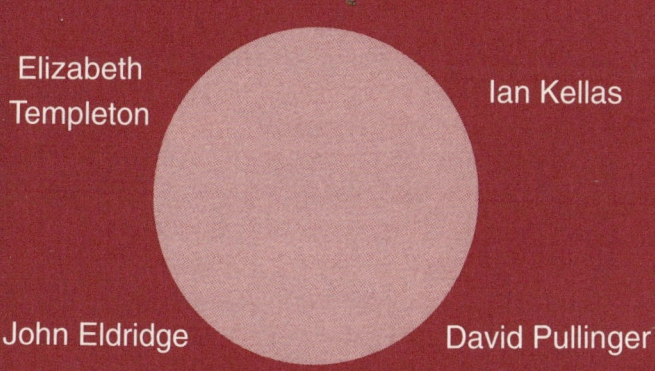

Tony Carty

Elizabeth Templeton

Ian Kellas

John Eldridge

David Pullinger

Malcolm Spaven

TALKING ABOUT TRIDENT

SOCIETY, RELIGION AND TECHNOLOGY PROJECT

First published in 1991 on behalf of
The SRT PROJECT of the
Church of Scotland Department of National Mission
by SAINT ANDREW PRESS
121 George Street, Edinburgh EH2 4YN

Copyright © SRT PROJECT 1991

ISBN 0 86153 148 5

All rights reserved. No part of this publication may be
reproduced or transmitted in any form or by any means,
electronic or mechanical, including photocopy, recording,
or information storage and retrieval system, without
permission in writing from the publisher. This book is
sold, subject to the condition that it shall not, by way of
trade or otherwise, be lent, re-sold, hired out or otherwise
circulated without the publisher's prior consent.

British Library Cataloguing in Publication Data
A catalogue record for this book
is available from the British Library.

Printed and bound by H K Clarkson & Sons Ltd,
Young Street, West Calder, West Lothian EH55 8EQ.

Contents

Acknowledgements
iv
Foreword
v
Talking about Trident
1
Afterword
89
References in Conversations
95
Contributors
96

Acknowledgements

Although this book is in the name of six people, there were two others whose involvement in earlier discussions we greatly appreciated. These are Helen Steven of the Iona Community and Peace House, Greenloaning, and Ronald Ferguson, parish minister in Kirkwall, Orkney. They also took the trouble to comment on early drafts of the manuscript and we thank them warmly for their help and encouragement.

Thanks are also due to Strategy (Scotland) Ltd for audio-transcription; to Morag Lyall for editorial assistance; to Saint Andrew Press; and to the Committee of the Society, Religion and Technology Project for supporting this initiative.

Foreword

British defence policy is back in the news. The discussions, however, have centred mainly on proposed cuts in the armed forces, with their attendant effects on military and civilian employment. In this book, our intention is to put the Trident nuclear missile system back on the public agenda.

In 1979, the newly elected Conservative government decided to replace Polaris submarines, the vehicles of Britain's independent nuclear deterrence policy, with Trident. This is not a simple replacement. The new missiles are many times more powerful than the old. It has been estimated that each of the four Trident submarines will carry weapons equivalent to 1,000 Hiroshima atom bombs. The missiles are also intended to be more accurate. So this modernisation of Britain's independent nuclear deterrent is quantitatively and qualitatively different from its predecessors.

In the 1970s and early 80s the wisdom of commissioning the Trident system was much questioned in parliament and in wider public debate. This went beyond the ranks of the peace movement, with military eminences such as Lord Carver maintaining that it would be suicidal to use Trident against the Soviet Union. But in recent years, once the decision was taken in parliament, contracts signed and work begun, things have been much quieter. The Labour Party, in opposition since 1979, has come to see its defence policy as a source of electoral vulnerability. Neil Kinnock is no longer associated with CND.

It remains the case that the Scottish National Party (SNP), Plaid Cymru and the Green Party are opposed to Trident. Yet, as Alex Salmond, leader of the SNP, recently pointed out: 'On defence policy, Labour has put itself in the remarkable position of being flanked on the left by the *Glasgow Herald* which recently questioned the rationale for the missile system.' (*Observer*, 28 July 1991)

The paradox is that, so far as the main parties are concerned, the political debate has frozen at a time when the world is manifestly changing. In the wake of Gorbachev's accession to power in the Soviet Union, the countries of Eastern Europe have moved out of monolithic communist control and out of Soviet hegemony. The Berlin Wall, symbol of the East-West divide, has come down and the Warsaw Pact has dissolved.

This was the impetus for setting up a discussion group under the auspices of the Church of Scotland's Society, Religion and Technology Project (SRT). In 1986, another discussion group, under the auspices of SRT produced the book *Ethics and Defence: Power and Responsibility in the Nuclear Age* (ed Davis). In the concluding paragraph of that study Davis wrote:

'The absolute priority for collective human responsibility for the future is to ensure that there will be a future and to combat those tendencies which threaten not just "ways of life", be they liberal, capitalist or socialist, but the continuity of life itself. While human action has always had and always will have hazards, the horror of our present situation is that human existence itself has become part of the calculus of risk. Recognition of this fact, when it does not lead to despair, can be a powerful driving force behind the search for an alternative to the *status quo*. It is the first step towards transcending the ideological and political divides of our time. Such thinking is imperative because of the high risks involved in standing still, and the even higher risks of allowing present trends to continue.'

So much has changed in the last five years, yet Britain's

policy of an independent nuclear deterrent remains in place. Why is this? A new discussion group was set up to explore this question. There was some overlap between the membership of the two groups. Essentially, however, we wanted to bring together a group that encompassed different crafts and disciplines of thought. In this case, it included art, computing science, defence studies, law, sociology and theology. We started with the concrete fact that Trident is to be based in Scotland. Faslane is a few miles down the Clyde from Glasgow and its conurbation. If Trident were based on the Thames then we might wonder about the feelings of Londoners if it was located at Tilbury. To have such powerful weapons of destruction in one's own back yard does, perhaps, provide some extra motivation for thinking about their presence. However that may be, our concern here is to explore Trident, not as a single issue, but in the context of the changing world scene. If there is a logic or illogic to the proposed deployment of Trident, then it is in a world context that it must be sought.

There is, we think, a cluster of questions which merit examination. At the political level, why have all post-war governments in Britain, Conservative and Labour, been wedded to a policy of nuclear deterrence? In particular, what are we to make of the concept of independent nuclear deterrence? In what circumstances could its independent use be contemplated? What does this tell us about Britain's relationship with the US? Are there limits to the trust we place in this special relationship? How does this connect with our collective membership of NATO? If Trident is a first-strike weapon, or perceived as such, where does that leave the theory of deterrence? If some military experts cannot see a feasible role for Trident, since

they regard its use as not credible, this raises questions about the status of deterrence language. Is it a matter of political rhetoric rather than military doctrine? Does this suggest that we are dealing with symbols of national greatness, with claims to great power status, rather than with defensible military logic? Can we continue to hold on to a concept of nuclear deterrence, even at the level of rhetoric, once the concept of the enemy and associated concepts of threat and conquest dissolve? What is the state of knowledge about the safety and the accuracy of the Trident missiles?

The members of the discussion group do share a scepticism about the role and appropriateness of Trident and we do not wish to disguise that. At the same time, we do not share the same theological positions and, in particular, some are pacifist and some are not. In what follows, we have constructed a text which we hope will be informative at a factual level and a stimulus to thought. There is an edited transcript of a new conversation which took place between members of the group on 11 May 1991, in Edinburgh. It is edited in that repetitions and unnecessary digressions have been cut. In places the sentence structure has also been simplified. But all the participants have seen this edited version and stand by their contributions. The text itself is interspersed by cartoons, all of which were done by Ian Kellas, and which are intended to highlight points made in the text. In addition, other material has been presented within a series of boxes throughout the book. This is intended to amplify or underline what is said in the conversation. Thus there are legal statements, chronologies, technical data and so on.

Where is the theology in all this, given that this is a Society, Religion and Technology project? Some of the discussion is explicitly theological—what kind of God do we relate to when we discuss issues of war and peace? But there is a proper sense in which the whole task is theological since the matter under discussion deals with issues of life and death. In a world of threat and menace, which the human species has made more dangerous and precarious, despite all the advances we might want to categorise under the name of progress, we put the question, what can we hope for?

In the Middle Ages, much more than now, Christians used to go on pilgrimage. As every reader of Chaucer knows, these could be very *human,* earthy affairs, not just pious spirituality. Such journeys were not only acts of faith but also opportunities for people to think about their lives and times. For us, this text represents a quest and we invite you, the reader, to share in our quest. Trident may seem a strange place of pilgrimage, but perhaps before long it will be a cultural relic if not a religious one. That is our hope. When that day comes then a modern pilgrimage would surely be in order—from Faslane to Holy Loch.

John Eldridge

Talking about Trident

John Eldridge: Within this group we have had a lot of discussion about Trident. We decided to meet and talk about this because we felt that the political debate had become frozen and because Trident, as Britain's latest independent nuclear deterrent, would be launched some time, we think, this year. We felt that it would be appropriate to look again at the issues surrounding this particular weapons system and ask ourselves what it is, why we have got it, and what we think it is supposed to do; also to try and see that particular weapons system in the context of wider discussions about the nuclear arms race, the arms race generally and problems of arms control. We have a local interest, of course, because Trident is going to be based on the Clyde and that is a stimulus for us to think about it as our near neighbour.

Elizabeth Templeton: The changes in the European scene in the last couple of years, which were beyond anybody's conception when the Trident programme began, have to be taken into account too as part of the shifting context of the discussion.

Tony Carty: A question I would like to put to Malcolm is that if, according to reports, the Polaris system is already worn out to the point where it is unusable and the Trident is supposed to come into operation in the late 1990s, then where are we situated at present with this independent nuclear defence system?

Malcolm Spaven: Yes, that is an interesting point because it seems to be an imperative for all governments in Britain that have supported nuclear weapons that Trident (or Polaris, at the moment) has to be out there twenty-four hours a day, seven days a week, 365 days a year, threatening Moscow all the time and if it's not, for even one second, somehow our security is deeply threatened. I think this is a very important issue: why is it that it has to be a 100% total system with absolutely no flaws? In the case of Polaris, I think the government is in a very difficult position because it is maintaining that there has never been one minute when there hasn't been at least one Polaris submarine on patrol. Some people have tried to dissect the wording and say, well what exactly do you mean by 'on patrol'? Does this simply mean that it is sitting in the harbour at Faslane but able to launch its missiles? Then it becomes rather ridiculous, the notion that if we don't have these missiles ready to fire at a few seconds' notice that somehow our whole society is going to crumble. On the more detailed technical point of Polaris falling apart, these are relatively old boats and it is well known that nuclear reactors don't perform well for much more than twenty-five years or so and you get increasing maintenance problems. Some of these submarines have been sitting in port for a long time now, apparently with reactor problems. Trident is not due in service until the mid 1990s so it does seem there is quite a chance of a gap between the withdrawal of Polaris and the introduction of Trident. How the government overcomes that, I don't know, but it seems to have successfully prevented anybody getting any hard evidence that the deterrent has failed.

Tony Carty: But presumably if it is clear that for a number of years there has been a nuclear defence gap and we have not been obliterated by the Soviets during those years, then that's the argument lost.

Malcolm Spaven: Well, I wonder. I think that's an interesting starting point for the whole business of people's feelings of insecurity. People are used to having these submarines patrolling and, before that, RAF bombers sitting on airfields armed with nuclear weapons ready to take off at a moment's notice. We still have, in terms of the technical organisation of the deterrent, the same system set up as we did at the height of the Cold War in the 1950s and early 1960s when, perhaps, people knew less about what was going on in the Soviet Union and the Soviet Union itself was a very different place. So it does seem extraordinary that we are doing exactly the same as we did thirty to forty years ago. But how will people react if it is shown that in fact there is this gap in the deterrent? Perhaps people's belief in Britain's nuclear weapons doesn't actually rely on there being an immediate and credible Soviet threat.

Tony Carty: I'd like to take up your point that we are continuing now as we did in the 1960s when the Soviet Union was definitely a different place. I was listening last week to a member of the Soviet Academy of Sciences, a Professor Wjaksheslaw Daschitschev, who was stating quite categorically that 1987 was a threshold point in Soviet history: that from 1920, when a decision was taken by the Soviet Communist Party to exclude all opposition, until 1987, the Soviet Union was definitely not a pluralist society. But since 1987 there has been an opening up of the society and, at present, there is a balance of power between the democratic forces behind Yeltsin and a more conservative traditional socialist or communist force behind Gorbachev. The country is struggling, he thought successfully, to attain a truly pluralist democratic sense of society. In Berlin, under hard questioning from a very sceptical German audience as to whether or not the Soviets were capable of democratic maturity, he pointed among other things to the miners' strikes and to what the miners were demanding. Then the miners were demanding economic autonomy and independence from central government planning, and this is precisely what Gorbachev accorded in early May. So I think we are faced with a theme which is the question of whether the Soviet Union has changed fundamentally in character. I would maintain that it definitely has, but this is something that I would like to come back to again and again. What may well not have changed are the attitudes of our own defence establishment.

Elizabeth Templeton: Yes, and I'm interested in whether there's a gap between the attitude of the defence establishment and the attitudes of the general population. I vividly remember, when we visited NATO headquarters on a previous occasion, being shocked beyond belief at what seemed to be the excess paranoia of the NATO people. It's clear, and documented in quite a lot of other European countries, that there is a real shift in general popular expectation, so that people don't feel this perpetual 'under threat' mentality as something that fits their own sense of how history is running. I wonder whether in Britain that's really been tested in the same way.

Ian Kellas: Can I come back? You have to argue that it's not just changed fundamentally, but irreversibly.

Tony Carty: Yes, well I've been doing my homework over the last ten days, going to one meeting after another. A meeting on the Soviet army that took place at the Polish Institute in Berlin suggested that the last time that the Soviet army could have been used to resolve tensions within Soviet society by some kind of external adventure would have been immediately after the end of the Afghanistan War and the withdrawal from Afghanistan. But the argument of the specialist Professor Galliss from Bremen at this meeting was very much that the army was thoroughly exhausted and demoralised by the Afghanistan War and that the military establishment doesn't see itself as being in a position to resolve the conflicts within the Soviet Union by undertaking foreign adventures. Since then, it's well known that the main security threat that the Soviet Union faces is the nationality conflict within its borders and the general consensus, from this fellow to Denis Healey and numerous others, is that the Army itself, as a Soviet army, reflects the ethnic divisions within the country and can't be expected to resolve them.

At the same time I come back to the point that the Russian professor made, that there is a stand-off between Yeltsin's forces and Gorbachev's forces. So there isn't a force within the Soviet Union that is capable of reversing the trends of the last four years. Any attempt to resolve the crisis in an authoritarian way would produce civil war. But Professor Daschitschev's view from the Soviet Academy of Sciences was primarily that there was a consensus among democratic forces on three essential points: first that there had to be a plural party system; second that the state monopoly of property had to be abolished; and third, that the nationalities had to be allowed to go their own way and that the Soviet Union had to be a voluntary confederation. Gorbachev has been known to resist all three of these and that is how the stand-off between the democrats and the Gorbachev conservatives has been seen. Fundamentally, Gorbachev is a liberal reformist within the communist framework. Since 1987 Gorbachev has formally accepted, in effect, the third point that the Union is going to be a voluntary confederation, and by handing over authority over natural resources to the individual states, particularly to Russia, he is in fact accepting an abandonment of state control of economic resources. He is resisting giving up the Communist Party monopoly but he has gone most of the way to accepting the democratic demands.

A further point that was stressed very strongly by this fellow was that the Communists have got no programme. There is a general consensus that in one way or another a market system must be introduced and that the idea that a central Moscow organisation, Gosplan, would be capable of managing the entire economy of the Soviet Union is no longer regarded as credible in any quarter. The Communists have got no other ideas about how to implement the process.

John Eldridge: Could I ask about this in terms of the notion of the arms race? I suppose, historically, there have been two general views about the Soviet Union. One is the classic idea about imperialist expansion, and the old communist texts were routinely trotted out when we wanted to justify the arms race because we wanted to prevent the spread of communist imperialism. The second, almost the opposite of that, is the notion of a society which is collapsing and is in a state of disarray—disintegration—and that in that situation another kind of danger arises. On the worst reading of this, in order to cope with all these internal stresses and strains, you have somehow to invent an external enemy: therefore even now we might hear some of the Soviet generals saying that NATO isn't playing fair in that it is going far beyond what was agreed on the modernisation and that the Soviets may have to rethink *their* position on modernisation. But the pessimistic argument would be that because the society is disintegrating, it might be that there would be some kind of military take-over and some kind of need for an external enemy in order to cope with internal weaknesses and fragmentation. Do you see what I am saying? These are two quite different arguments. My own opinion is that the first one, the notion of imperialist expansion, is the one that traditionally has fuelled the whole business of the arms race. But I suppose, if you want to hold on to a nuclear deterrent, you might bring the second one into play on the grounds that you really don't quite know what's going to happen in a period of such rapid change, which we all hope will go in democratic pluralist directions, but might collapse upon itself and then lead to some sort of authoritarian militarist régime which would carry with it its own threats: perhaps a Russian threat even more than a Soviet threat, who knows?

Malcolm Spaven: I think that is a really interesting point because that brings us into the whole business of thinking about the role of the military in society, in the Soviet Union in this case, but also I think we ought to extend that to looking at the role of the military in society in this country and in the United States. The Red Army has always played a very important social and political role in the Soviet Union. The historical memory of the Red Army's role in the Second World War is still very powerful so the people who hang on to traditional views of the Soviet state and who support many of the old policies, who opposed Gorbachev from the start and have a great affinity with the Red Army and its traditional role—those people still have considerable power. They see the army, or the military in general, as a kind of 'glue' of Soviet society in a period when it's in a state of collapse or disintegration. They feel the need to have an institution that represents security, that represents continuity and tradition—something that they can hang on to in a period of uncertainty.

It's more obvious perhaps in the Soviet Union but I think it's also true in this country, though to a much lesser degree. Partly because we weren't defeated in war, I think the military is held in fairly high esteem in our country and most of the images that are presented of the military are very positive. People have a kind of warm feeling about the armed forces: they remember the Battle of Britain, they remember all the positive contribution that the military made during the Second World War, and I think people like to hang on to that. Perhaps in the last ten years in this country, when there has been a period of very rapid social change, maybe people feel the need, as they do in the Soviet Union, for an institution that represents security, tradition and continuity. I think that is a very important factor in the whole debate about Polaris and Trident and the fact that Trident in particular embodies continuity and tradition. It embodies total security, it's never failed: it's there every minute of every day. Even while we sleep it's there training its missiles on Moscow just in case we are attacked.

Elizabeth Templeton: But I wonder if that really does reflect British feeling at the moment. I am not sure when the last testing or sounding of British public opinion on Trident was done, but, as I understand it, most people a few years back were not being persuaded by this myth of the necessity of constant vigilance against a sinister enemy. Trident did not have such massive popular backing, so I am a bit doubtful about whether this focus on the military in popular sentiment as an agent of stability is really as strong as you are suggesting.

Malcolm Spaven: Well, I would say two things on that: one is that I don't think it's necessarily tied to the need for an external enemy. I think this is one of the interesting things about it. The Soviet case illustrates that very clearly. I don't believe that most people in the Soviet Union think that the West is about to attack them—other than perhaps economically—but they feel the need for something which will help society to remain integrated, and I think in this country we are now getting into that realm as well. I agree with you that several years ago, for some time, people really didn't think that Trident was a terribly good idea, but if you asked them a different question, which was, 'Do you believe that Britain needs to retain its nuclear weapons?' there would be an overwhelming 'Yes' to that and I think that still remains the case. I personally think that that felt need in the British people has more to do with their vision of British society internally, domestically, than it does with the threat of war. I think that people need to have an institution which represents something terribly definite when all around them things are in the process of really quite rapid change.

Ian Kellas: What occurs to me is if it is mainly to do with creating an image? It's more socially cohesive to have a picture of our boys parachuting in to wherever with their guns blazing. You can't parade a tartan Trident up and down the High Street or have shows of nuclear warheads in Holyrood Park.

Malcolm Spaven: But it's the ultimate certainty. This is the official position, isn't it? It's the ultimate certainty, whereas if you send our boys into some kind of conventional war, in a sense that's the failure of deterrence. What you have in Trident is a guarantee, according to the official position, that there will never

Public Opinion on Trident

Opinion polls between 1980 and 1984 consistently found that a majority of people were opposed to the government's plans to purchase Trident to replace Polaris. These ranged from 52% against Trident in a Marplan poll for the BBC's *Panorama* programme in September 1980, 59% against in a Marplan/*Weekend World* poll two weeks later, 56% against in a Gallup/CND poll in October 1982 and a Marplan/*Guardian* poll in January 1983, to as many as 63% against in a Gallup poll for CND on 28 May 1984.

From the mid-1980s, opinion appeared to be more evenly balanced, but even as late as 1988 there was little evidence of absolute majority support for Trident. A Policy Research Associates poll in that year found 46% in favour of Trident, 37% against, and 17% unsure.

[*Glasgow Herald*, 5 April 1988]

Scotland has shown deeper hostility to Trident. A System 3 poll commissioned by Scottish CND on 13 May 1987 found that, in the event of the United States and the Soviet Union agreeing to withdraw medium-range missiles from Europe, only 23% of Scots were in favour of the British government continuing with the acquisition of Trident.

Opinion polls have also demonstrated some of the contradictions inherent in nuclear deterrence. A Gallup poll for Bradford University School of Peace Studies just before the 1987 general election found that, while 67% would be unhappy with a world in which only the United States and the Soviet Union had nuclear weapons (implying 67% supported British possession of nuclear weapons), only 55% specifically supported a British independent nuclear force.

The same poll also demonstrated that public support for British possession of nuclear weapons does not necessarily indicate that people are prepared to accept the logic of deterrence. Of those asked, 69% said they were opposed to the launching of Polaris missiles against the Soviet Union as a last-ditch defence against a Soviet attack on the UK. So while a majority may believe in retaining British nuclear weapons, an even greater proportion is not prepared to sanction the use which underpins the credibility of those weapons as a deterrent.

[*Glasgow Herald*, 11 June 1987]

be any serious threat to Britain itself. I mean, sending the boys in is all very well but it all happens thousands of miles away. It doesn't actually affect British society except to reinforce that positive image. I am not trying to argue that there is some contradiction between supporting our boys in the Gulf or in the Falklands or wherever it might be on the one hand, and the idea of nuclear based security on the other. I think in a sense they reinforce each other and they are part of the same thing, which is this generally positive image of the military in society. It's regarded as an institution that represents certain kinds of values that people feel positive about, and Trident is one aspect of that.

Ian Kellas: I suppose what I am trying to get at is, if I was a politician and I was picking up on what you said about the military having this positive image, I would want to exploit that somehow, but there would still be a separate question about whether Trident is actually effective any longer in practical military terms. Then if I had decided that it wasn't really, I might well be prepared to scrap it—given that it is very expensive. So I would want to disentangle the mythical side of its function from its strategic purposes. Looking at its strategic purposes I would want to know: is it a very particular kind of weapon, is it really just designed to terrorise people in Moscow or can it be used in other situations that are more likely to occur now?

John Eldridge: What sort of situations?

Ian Kellas: Like, say, supposing civil war does break out in the Soviet Union or supposing Saddam Hussein had got away in the Middle East and had overrun the Gulf.

John Eldridge: I hear what you say but I don't see where it takes us. We would launch a Trident missile into the Middle East—into Iraq?

The Costs of Trident

Total capital cost of the UK Trident programme £9,863 million (at 1990-91 prices).[1] This figure represents a reduction in real terms of £1,838 million (19%) from the original estimate for Trident II in March 1982, but an increase of some 25% over the original estimate for the smaller Trident I system in 1980. 30% of the UK Trident budget will be spent in the United States.

However, the official figure only includes:

- Capital Costs. The costs of building the submarines, missiles, warheads and shore facilities, but not the cost of operating the system once it has been built.
- 'Attributable' Costs. Some facilities for the Trident project —notably the shore construction at Faslane and Rosyth, development of a new nuclear power reactor, and the sonar system—will also be used by other submarines. Re-development of the nuclear warhead production facilities at Aldermaston is also designed to support production of other warheads after Trident is built. The government has therefore only attributed some of those costs to the Trident project.

Greenpeace has identified more than £2,500 million in Trident-related expenditure which has not been included in the official price tag for Trident.[2]

The Ministry of Defence says it gives a 'high priority' to life-cycle costing (estimating the costs of operating and maintaining equipment, as well as the cost of building it).[3] But the official government estimate for Trident excludes the operating costs of the system entirely. Greenpeace has estimated them to amount to more than £10,000 million over the life of the Trident system, at 1990-91 prices.

Adding 'Trident-related' capital expenditure, and the costs of operating Trident, would more than double the overall bill, to £23,000 million.[4]

---

[1] [House of Commons Written Answer, 12 February 1991]

[2] [Greenpeace UK, *The Problems of the Trident Programme*, July 1991, p ix]

[3] [Evidence to House of Commons Defence Committee, *The Reliability and Maintainability of Defence Equipment*, HC40, 1990, p xvi]

[4] [Greenpeace UK, *op. cit.* p viii]

Ian Kellas: That's what I am asking really—whether Trident has any strictly functional purpose. If the traditional Soviet threat is removed, does it have any, or does it only have a mythical purpose?

Malcolm Spaven: Well, I would argue that the mythical side of it is much more important than the practical side which has less and less content nowadays. I think there are important points here about the nature of deterrence. If the Soviet threat is not there any more, what or who, in practical terms, will Trident be deterring?

Elizabeth Templeton: I am interested in how long the myth can actually survive or even is surviving, because I think that the government is having to work harder and harder to pull the wool over people's eyes. I think the fact that we are on the edge of going into some kind of more integrated European vision is going to make it more and more impossible for Britain to take this kind of lofty isolation—its heroic little empire view of itself—and we are already very clearly far down on the lists in terms of things like ecological responsibility and so on in relation to the rest of Europe. It seems to me that what is going to be happening in the next few years, certainly the next few decades, is that the whole world community will have to recognise that the only possible kind of future is going to be a collaborative one, or else the planet is not going to be there; if national military strategy has to be put in that context I just don't see how we can really think people are going to go on buying this story of their fate being bound up with something like this kind of deterrent.

John Eldridge: Let's go back to the point that Ian has raised because we are all clear that the official justification for nuclear deterrents generally, and Trident in particular, has to do with the Soviet Union. If we were to pursue your question, what we would have to be saying would be that we can invent another function for this weapons system which was not in our minds originally; we would have not only to invent it but would have to feel that it was justified in a practical way and I think that would be very difficult. I have not seen any attempt to do that. So my view is that you have got to get back to the Soviet Union, and that that is where the heart of the discussion is.

Ian Kellas: What about China for instance?

Tony Carty: Well, China is a country whose particular form of nationalist arrogance seems to be an indifference to the rest of the world—a sort of isolation of just one Chinese world with no reason to believe that China has any aspirations to dominate the planet. That's not its tradition. Its tradition is to regard itself as the planet and everything else outside China is a matter of very little consequence.

John Eldridge: I just want to try and nail this thing about the Soviet Union because—

Tony Carty: Under questioning, this professor said that the consensus in the Soviet establishment was that there had been an adequate Western response to the liberalisation in the Soviet Union and an adequate Western response to the Soviet withdrawal from Eastern Europe and disbandment of the Warsaw Pact. It was that the NATO Alliance had formally declared that the Soviet Union was no longer regarded as an enemy. This was last July.

To come back to another meeting that I attended in Berlin on defence questions in the post-Gulf context, the speaker from the Christian Democratic Union, and the governing party's Foreign Relations Committee, Lammer, stated in a meeting, at which there were on the platform, pacifist, green and radical left-wing political speakers, his view—that Germany was under no threat from any quarter as far as he could see. Then he hesitated for quite a while and said, 'The only possible conceivable threat that could arise some time in the near future' —and this raised eyebrows in the audience—'would be Islamic fundamentalism in the political situation in the Middle East.' But he was definitely confirming the consensus within the Christian Democratic Union that there was no security problem in Europe. This is very much a popular political pronouncement, not an academic, strategic think-tank pronouncement. The discussion in Germany about Germany's international role is having a great deal of difficulty getting off the ground because an opinion poll, conducted in Germany at the beginning of this year about Germany's role in the world, confirms that the vast majority of the Germans modelled themselves on Sweden and Switzerland as ideal political societies. In other words, they are not willing to accept that they have any significant role to play in the world.

I would like to come on to two or three points that arise out of what Malcolm and Elizabeth have been saying. Discussion about defence and discussion about deterrence is a discussion about perceptions. What I have just been talking about is, I believe, a fairly accurate account of how the Germans see themselves in the centre of Europe at the moment. After all, if there was to be a Soviet threat and it was to hit Germany first then the United Kingdom would always be involved only on the basis of collective security and the fact that it had to come in to assist other NATO members. The French, if you like left-wing *Le Monde diplomatique*, view of British-American military strategy is very much that the United States and the United Kingdom

> The Commander of the US Navy's Submarine Fleet in the Atlantic told a Florida-based newspaper in January 1990 that the changes in East-West relations gave Trident a role as 'a defence against terrorism, drug trading and other global conflicts.'
>
> [Vice-Admiral Roger Bacon, (Commander, Submarines, US Atlantic Fleet), quoted in *Times-Union* (Jacksonville, Florida), 20 January 1990]

suffer very severe economic problems—the United Kingdom's economic problems are chronic—and that is the source of the threat to their national security. These countries have compensated for some time, and I'm thinking of the United States, by specialising in arms technology, in the arms trade, in the arms industry. The argument is that these two countries intend to compensate against the real enemy which is not the Soviet Union, which is well on the way to becoming an insignificant peripheral power on the very borders of Europe, but Germany and Japan, which constitute lethal economic threats to the United States and to the United Kingdom. So the function of the military industrial complex in the United Kingdom and the United States is to put pressure on Germany and Japan, to divert energy and resources into supporting this complex as a kind of world policing; and you have the astronomical pressure on Germany and Japan to pay for the Gulf War as evidence of this future trend. So I would say that there's a real danger, given the underlying deep economic and social tension in the United States and the United Kingdom, that constitutes a threat to international security.

Elizabeth Templeton: That seems to be quite convincing. I share that view, but how does the episode arise, for example, about Gorbachev having said that if American attitudes towards the Soviet Union didn't change then there might be a return to a kind of Cold War situation? Now, what's going on there: is that our media trying to put Gorbachev down or is it something else? I just don't understand that.

Ian Kellas: Yes, what I'm trying to establish is what a worst case scenario might look like.

John Eldridge: But what would this worst case scenario look like? Would it mean that there's some potential for the Soviet Union to feel threatened? After all, it could be argued that through the Gorbachev initiatives the wind-down on arms control took place: a lot of the initiatives came from the Soviet Union, and there have been responses from the West. But if the feeling continues that perhaps the West isn't doing its bit, but that in the name of modernisation, of which Trident is a small part, we are actually still sustaining a very hostile stance towards the Soviet Union, then is there any sense in which the notion of the Soviet threat, which maybe we ourselves in the West would help to engender, is something that we would feel we would still have to counter in some ways? Now, I'm putting that as a worst case scenario. There's a difference in that from the traditional one which is about the spread of communism in the world.

Tony Carty: We have really to get to grips with the nature of the so-called thinking that goes on around deterrents and, indeed, military strategy. The worst case scenario is an entirely subjective concept: it's the individual who imagines himself to be threatened and conceives of the worst possible thing that could possibly happen to him and then sets out to provide some kind of mechanism to defend himself against that. But that's quite dif-

> Nothing in the present Charter shall impair the inherent right of individual or collective self-defence if an armed attack occurs against a Member of the United Nations.
> [The Charter of the United Nations, 1945, Article 51]

ferent from foreign policy analysis of what's actually going on in another country and I think a lawyer looking at when self-defence would be justified in international law would want some evidence which constitutes a reasonable ground for believing that the other side actually constitutes a threat. There, I simply don't see what the evidence is supposed to be. I don't see how a Soviet military take-over would be thought of, within the Soviet Union, as a way of solving the radically outdated and backward nature of the Soviet economy. I don't see how the Soviet army, given that it is a multinational force, is supposed to be able to respond through some kind of Pinochet action to nationality conflicts within the Soviet Union. The point has been made that up until now in the Baltic context that the Red Army's not been used. They've used rather dubious quasi-militial forces of the Department of the Interior within the Soviet Union. I think the evidence has got to be produced.

I think that with respect to Elizabeth's comment about the Gorbachev statement any possible number of analyses can be

raised. Gorbachev is very concerned about being written off by the Americans and the Americans dealing directly with Yeltsin. He's very concerned about the too-forward American policy towards the Baltic states. He still hopes that he can treat this as some kind of internal arrangement. I think the crisis within the Soviet Union has to be described more precisely, and the crisis again is a matter of perception. We, who are used to a Soviet Union in which one man speaks for the entire nation, become very concerned if we find two or three Soviets publicly in disagreement. We are, ourselves, unable to adjust to the notion of pluralism within the Soviet Union and, given the nature of our own political society, where we cannot tolerate dissension in public about any matter within any public organisation, whether it's a Church or the army or political party, it is we who have the difficulty in handling conflict in other countries.

I would maintain that analysis of what is happening in the Soviet Union at the moment has to take into account the widely accepted and respected analysis of Paul Kennedy about the nature of over-stretched military power. The Russian professor I mentioned said that Stalin took a wrong turn after the war when he insisted that the Soviet Union should set itself up in confrontation against the entire world. In other words there was a reasonable American and British anxiety about Soviet intentions in the 1940s and 1950s, but that it's now realised within the Soviet Union, accepting the kind of analysis of Paul Kennedy, that it is not up to it. It hasn't got the capacity to undertake this confrontational process and Helmut Schmidt points out that the genius of Gorbachev is to retreat gracefully. It's simply to accept that the foreign policy strategies of the Soviet Union, which are the legacy of Stalin, are completely beyond the resources of the country.

The Yeltsin phenomenon then is interpreted as—in a sense it's quite an egocentric and unconstructive development in the Soviet Union—a kind of Russian impatience with carrying the burden of the rest of the empire. Why should they be responsi-

> Paul Kennedy argues that great political and economic powers such as Spain, France and Britain, and now the US and the USSR, have all overstretched themselves militarily. In this way they have dragged themselves down. The example is clearest with the British empire and now appears to be the case when the US accept military responsibilities to maintain world peace which are beyond its financial resources.
>
> [Paul M Kennedy, *The Rise and Fall of the Great Powers: Economic Change and Military Conflict from 1500 to 2000*, Fontana, 1989]

ble for these Asian, Muslim provinces which are even more backward than they are? Why should they be bothered with these extremely troublesome Armenians and Georgians who are tearing one another's guts out? Well, let them get on with it. The Russians have demanded the handing over of natural resources to the individual states. Now, more than half the resources of the Soviet Union are within the Russian Federation, so there's very much an intention by the Russians, as represented by Yeltsin, to get on with it and look after themselves. So, I come back to my fundamental point: what's the evidence that the so-called disintegration of the Soviet Union constitutes a threat?

John Eldridge: Well, I think this is very important, isn't it? It goes back to the point I was making earlier, that if we recognise that the old enemy Soviet imperialism is now totally off the agenda, we then look to the alternative threat which is about disintegration in the USSR leading to the need for an external enemy. If we now argue that we don't have any kind of evidence of this alternative Soviet or Russian threat, should it involve us in the establishment of nuclear weapons? It seems to me that is a very fundamental point. If we're saying that the 'Soviet threat' is part of the argument, in the end what we're dealing with is a cultural relic. But it happens to be a pretty dangerous cultural relic, because there are safety problems and other kinds of problems about it as well: for example, economic issues ...

Elizabeth Templeton: I'm still exploring your worst case fantasy, as it were. I don't know whether things are going to change on the current international debate, which you must be very much alive to, about what counts as legitimate interference by one country in another country's internal affairs. I think that there's a blurred area at the moment because what has counted as internal affairs is now becoming questioned in various contexts, most noticeably the Kurdish one. But I wonder whether my worst case fantasy might be that the present Soviet Union blows up over the ethnic question and that there is an attempt to put down ethnic unrest by military means, which I know you're saying wouldn't work. But supposing they tried it and made a real mess of it, then I wonder whether it's not also a possibility that, for all the reasons we've mentioned about American insecurity internally, there might not be another attempt by the United States to say, 'Right, in our role as world policemen we cannot allow this kind of thing to happen. Let us give them a salutary lesson.' Now, that's my worst case, I think, which would be allowing the US military government machine to make a pretext out of Soviet misbehaviour. I don't know whether there's any way Trident could be invoked in that kind of situation, but unless we can scotch that one I still have a little edge of nightmare that it could be abused in that way.

Malcolm Spaven: But the irony of that situation would be that that would be an example of Soviet nuclear deterrence failing miserably.

Elizabeth Templeton: Right.

Malcolm Spaven: You could argue that your scenario is that the Soviet Union ceased to exist anyway, so, therefore, you can't have Soviet deterrence. That does lead us on to the other

Safety Concerns

Serious misgivings about the safety of the Trident warhead and missile have been expressed by an expert commission set up by the US Congress. The Drell Commission, which reported in December 1990[1], found that the US Navy had made a deliberate decision in 1983 not to incorporate a number of safety features in the design of the warhead for Trident.

The 1983 decision had been dictated by a desire to achieve maximum range with the maximum number of warheads on each missile. To do so, the Navy decided to use a type of high explosive (used to trigger the nuclear explosion) and a type of propellant (rocket fuel) which are sensitive to impact—they can explode simply by being struck. The safer Insensitive High Explosive then available would have taken up too much room in the missile and forced the Navy to reduce either the number or yield of the warheads. Use of less sensitive rocket fuel would have reduced the range of the missiles.

The 1983 decision also involved arranging the warheads around one of the rocket motors, instead of on top as is usually the practice. In addition, only limited fire protection was given to the nuclear cores of the warheads.

The result, according to Drell, is that there is a risk that detonation of the rocket fuel could in turn cause an explosion of the high explosive in the warhead, and the result could be a dispersal of the plutonium in the warhead.

The British Trident system will use the same missiles as those in the US Navy. Although the exact configuration of the British warhead is still secret, the evidence strongly suggests that it will be virtually identical to the American design. The Drell Commission's safety concerns are therefore of considerable relevance to Britain's Trident missiles.

When the House of Commons Defence Committee attempted to assess the implications of the Drell Report for the safety of Britain's Tridents, they were met with what they have described as 'bland assurances combined with apparent attempts to deflect attention from the issue.'[2]

Drell had noted that the simple expedient of replacing the third-stage rocket fuel with a less sensitive type would eliminate the worst dangers of a missile-handling accident, with only a 100-150 mile reduction in the missile's range. The House of Commons Defence Committee made the same point interesting point the whole of the West's nuclear deterrence policy is based on the premise of a completely integrated and monolithic Soviet Union. Britain's actually a better illustration of this than American policy—ever since Polaris was introduced, we've had a policy which is based on attacking Moscow—nothing else. I've never seen any evidence that Britain's ever targeted anything else. It would be difficult to, technically. So Trident is based on the ability to credibly threaten Moscow, through all the anti-ballistic missile defences. This is one of the main reasons the government argues that you need more warheads. But if the Soviet Union has collapsed then presumably the threat doesn't necessarily come from Moscow. You might get into a situation where the threat in your worst case scenario doesn't come from Moscow at all but from, say, a rebel republic, and the people who are doing the threatening might actually be quite pleased if someone dropped a nuclear bomb on Moscow.

Ian Kellas: But, Malcolm, you're not seriously suggesting that they couldn't target some other city in the Soviet Union?

Malcolm Spaven: In practical terms I think it would be very difficult. It's probably less difficult with Trident than it was with Polaris, but the job of re-targeting a missile is immensely complex, even with something modern like the Cruise missile. Until very recently it took them a long time (it could be days or weeks) to get the information into a missile that would re-target it. Basically, the missile has a computer in it that is loaded with the data for a specific target and in order to change all that data and change all the settings in the inertial guidance of the missile, to have the maps that they would need, the data on the magnetic environment and so on: they may not have that data for other targets. The Americans may well do, but whether the British do is completely another matter. And so, in a sense, we're technically locked in to attacking Moscow, but if Moscow is

Safety Concerns (cont'd)

to the MoD. But the Committee found that the Ministry of Defence had not seriously looked at safer missile designs because it could not afford to add UK-specific requirements to a missile being purchased off-the-shelf from the USA.

The other problem for the MoD is that any changes to warhead design at this stage would delay the missile's entry into service, possibly leading to a gap in the operation of the British nuclear deterrent between the retiral of Polaris and the introduction of Trident.

[1] [Nuclear Weapons Safety: Report of the Panel on Nuclear Weapons Safety of the Committee on Armed Services, House of Representatives, Committee Print No15, US Government Printing Office, December 1990]

[2] [House of Commons Defence Committee, *The Progress of the Trident Programme,* HC 286, July 1991, p xi]

ceasing to become as relevant as it was then this is a kind of hole in our deterrence policy.

Elizabeth Templeton: But, supposing it still was Moscow, just for my worst case argument to be explored, that was trying to keep someone else down so that it was still credible to the British and the American moral mapping of the situation to say Moscow is the baddie.

Tony Carty: Well, I think there we can come back to fairly safe ground and say that it has never been the intention of either the British or the Americans to use nuclear weapons as an instrument of national policy. It's always been a last case resort to defend the existence of the United States and the United

Kingdom, but the British argument for having these weapons is that the Americans would not use them just to defend the United Kingdom against a threat. This is certainly the French view as well, and in the bad old Cold War days it was the German view that the problem would be coupling. So I think that the likelihood of the Americans using nuclear weapons to teach the Soviets a lesson is ridiculous.

Malcolm Spaven: But surely it's not a question of whether they would use them or not, surely the important question from the point of view of the government is: 'Are there actions which a separatist movement in the Soviet Union, or for that matter the Red Army or a conservative faction in the Soviet Union, might want to take but which they will not take because they know that Britain and America have nuclear weapons?' That's the real question.

Tony Carty: But I think the answer to that is definitely no.

Malcolm Spaven: I agree. I think, particularly after the Gulf War, it's far more likely that there would be some kind of intervention with conventional weapons, if it got to the use of military force. That is a far more credible deterrent, if you like, although the fact they have to use the force means it's not a deterrent. That's far more credible than any possession of nuclear weapons.

Tony Carty: It has to be said that the general Western policy, and particularly the European policy at the moment, has not been to encourage secessionist movements within the Soviet Union and it has really been, as it has always been in international relations, traditionally conservative. The attempt has been to retain the existing territorial entities of the international system, including the Soviet Union. We've seen it in Iraq. I mean, the Americans don't want formally to admit the notion of

The Official British Position

During the Cold War

Non-nuclear war between East and West is by far the likeliest road to nuclear war. We must therefore seek to prevent any war, not just nuclear war, between East and West ... in essence we seek to ensure that whatever military aggression or political bullying a future Soviet leader might contemplate, he could not foresee any likely situation in which the West would be left with no realistic alternative to surrender.

[Statement on the Defence Estimates 1981]

As long as the basic tensions between East and West are undiminished, NATO will need to continue to rely on a strategy of nuclear deterrence based on an effective mix of systems. Nuclear weapons will remain as vital for keeping the peace—for preventing conventional and well as nuclear war in Europe —as they have been for the past forty years.

[Statement on the Defence Estimates 1987, p 14]

After the Cold War

Now, I'd say this, because there is a feeling I think that nuclear weapons somehow haven't proved their worth: this is the triumph, what we are seeing now, of the nuclear deterrent. We're seeing a transformation in Eastern Europe, coming with freedom and democracy breaking out right across that part of the European continent, and a real triumph for the values that we cherish in the West: democracy and freedom against the destruction and evil of communism. That's been achieved without a single life being lost.

[Tom King, Defence Secretary,
BBC Radio 4, *The World This Weekend*, 13 May 1990]

Unless you have a nuclear deterrent capability, a strategic nuclear capability, you are not properly defended.

[Alan Clark MP, Minister for Defence,
BBC Radio 4, *Today*, 31 May 1990]

When one looks at the wider world, one sees that the biggest problem at present, which no doubt worries the Soviet Union as well as the Western powers, is the degree of proliferation and the variety of missile and warhead capabilities. There is no doubt that we need to consider those aspects when looking at our defence plans.

[Tom King, Defence Secretary, House of Commons debate on Defence Estimates, 18 June 1990] a separate Kurdistan; even in the context of Saddam Hussein, they're very anxious to maintain existing territorial entities. This is the dominant international law and received wisdom of international political élites concerned with international affairs. Yugoslavia, in fact, is the test case of the law because it seems to be breaking up and the West is uncertain about what kind of attitude to adopt towards Yugoslavia which does not constitute a precedent affecting its very conservative attitude towards the Soviet Union. Yeltsin was very badly treated when he turned up at Strasburg at the European Parliament. I think the general consensus among the liberal, political élites in Europe is to favour Gorbachev as far as possible. So, I think—

Ian Kellas: I can see, then, a motive for keeping Trident because nuclear weapons probably serve to keep this whole kind of state edifice intact.

Tony Carty: I would say that the real threat to peace and security, going back to what Elizabeth was saying, really comes from the Anglo-American military establishment. I think that is appreciated in France, in Japan and among the Social Democrats in the centre left of Germany. That at a structural level the economic weakness and social contradictions that affect British and American society are much deeper than those of the other countries that are threatened in terms of their economic survival. There's a House of Lords Report that I was looking at in the context of an Economic and Social Research Council study group on the legitimacy of the British state which points out that in the course of the 1990s there could be a crisis of democracy in Britain because the political institutions will be faced with an inability to implement a consensus on social policy, given the steady and apparently irreversible decline in the British economy. The one compensation is in the military context. That's at the structural level.

At the more micro level there is deep concern within French

The British Position (cont'd)

The United Kingdom's strategic deterrent makes an important contribution to alliance security and is the ultimate guarantee of our security—an insurance policy against unwelcome developments in the future. Trident will allow us to maintain a credible strategic nuclear deterrent well into the next century at a relatively modest cost and we remain entirely convinced of the need for it.

[Archie Hamilton, Defence Minister, House of Commons debate on the Defence Estimates, 19 June 1990]

Trident and the Gulf War

If Iraq developed nuclear weapons who can seriously doubt that he [Saddam Hussein] would have used them? ... A Conservative government will not throw away or bargain away our nuclear weapons while other countries have them.

[Chris Patten, Chairman of the Conservative Party, speech to Annual Young Conservatives Conference, Scarborough, 9 February 1991]

Trident and Arms Control

The introduction of Trident in the mid-1990s will provide the minimum capability necessary to maintain an effective independent deterrent into the next century and the reductions in prospect [in US and Soviet strategic nuclear arsenals] would not reduce our strategic needs ... Our independent strategic nuclear force remains the cornerstone of our defence capability.

[Statement on the Defence Estimates 1991, p 35]

The United Kingdom's position on the role of our own nuclear deterrent in strategic negotiations remains that, if Soviet and US strategic arsenals were to be very substantially reduced and if no significant changes had occurred in Soviet defensive capabilities, we would want to consider how we could best contribute to arms control in the light of the reduced threat. But US and Soviet reductions would have to go much further than 50% before we could consider including the British deterrent in arms control negotiations.

[Statement on the Defence Estimates 1988, p 14]

and German, maybe left of centre, intellectual circles that came up in the meeting in Berlin on alternative defence strategies, at which the CDU spokesman Lammer was present, that the decision making process within the United States' political establishment is alarming. It's imperial. In the Roman style. It consists of the cronies, usually life-time political buddies who happen to be hanging around the President. Whatever sophistication the American military establishment may reach in terms of its scientific and technological expertise, whatever expertise there may be in American think-tanks and in élite American universities and institutions, they do not impinge directly on the way the United States takes international security decisions. These are taken by Bush with his political cronies in the White House —people who are not necessarily institutionally responsible to Congress—maybe his campaign manager, his head of staff. If you look into the decision-making process with respect to the conduct of the Gulf War it does seem to be very irrational, very much based on hunches and gut feelings about Saddam and what has to be done about Saddam and getting Saddam and so on, and not working out the consequences, even in the worst case scenario of a highly technocratic militaristic style.

This comes back to the point Elizabeth was making a few moments ago about Trident: where does Britain situate itself in this context, because Britain is very much the lapdog of the United States in terms of the decision-making? The argument there is that Trident would commit the United Kingdom very much to this rather irrational, in the sense of unpredictable and not clearly explicable, American decision-making process. Helmut Schmidt pushes for the stabilising force in the world having to be a European military power. Given the collapse of the Soviet Union, given the disappearance of the Soviet Union from the international system, what force can balance against this irrational and unrestricted military power within the United States? The only force, given that people have to continue thinking in terms of balance of power, and force and strategic offsets, is a

Nuclear Decision-Making

Following a four-year study of the individuals, institutions and mechanisms of nuclear decision-making, the Oxford Research Group (ORG) concluded that the decision-making structures in all the nuclear weapon-possessing states 'have a dynamic of their own'. Decisions were taken by 'a maze of committees whose deliberations are secret ... whose names are little known ... [and which are] subject to little real accountability'.[1]

Despite growing public concern about the escalating nuclear arms race since the 1970s, the potential restraints on nuclear weapons decisions, through legislative bodies, informed public opinion, financial scrutiny and arms control, had 'yet to prove as strong as the forces driving the arms race'.

One the major obstacles to change identified by ORG was that 'in the West the tendency has been for power to accrue to the permanent bureaucracies, the nuclear laboratories and the military services, which have the institutional continuity to see projects through from beginning to end. The politicians come and go rapidly and lack the power to make decisions stick if the bureaucracies oppose them.'[2]

ORG found ten specific factors underpinning British nuclear weapons decision-making:

1. Nuclear research is highly classified, preventing proper peer review and eliminating moral questions from consideration.
2. Threat assessments on which nuclear weapons decisions are based cannot be verified by ministers, parliament, or the public. Threats are often exaggerated, and the data presented in a distorted fashion, in order to support particular weapons programmes.
3. Defence procurement contracts are insufficiently controlled; costs are often allowed to escalate.
4. Permanent officials, who play a key role in the continuity of nuclear weapons programmes, are not sufficiently accountable.
5. The Treasury has insufficient resources and political clout to monitor and control defence spending.

European political-military power. The pressure then coming from France and Germany is that there should be some military union as part of the unification process in Western Europe. There Britain is faced with a challenge: does it go in to this process or does it try to have a schizophrenic existence whereby its economic unity is supposed to rest in Europe and its military-political unity rests with the United States?

Ian Kellas: This European force is meant to be non-nuclear, is it?

Tony Carty: Well, you have to get down to detail and there Germany is committed in its treaty with the Soviet Union, the unification treaty of November 1990, to remaining a non-nuclear power, so basically the nuclear forces that Britain and France have would have to remain outside any kind of German political authority.

Malcolm Spaven: On the other hand, here's the potential new role for British nuclear weapons, because the German forces —I'm not suggesting this is necessarily a likelihood, but it's a possibility—have access to American nuclear weapons and it's quite widespread throughout the German air force in particular. If the Americans were pulling out of Europe and there was the creation of a new European force, why is it not possible for Britain to replace America as the provider of nuclear weapons to German, or pan-European, forces?

I think the real barrier is that Britain would never agree to hand over its weapons, even under custodial power, to the Germans and that illustrates just how powerfully nationalistic our nuclear weapons policy is.

John Eldridge: Can I just go back to Tony saying that the big risk was from the United States and the UK rather than from the Soviet Union. The question I'm asking is what kind of threat

Nuclear Decision-Making (cont'd)

6. The Foreign Office has insufficient say in future weapons decisions. Arms control has a low priority; defence policy dictates foreign policy.
7. Nuclear weapons agreements with the United States are shrouded in secrecy.
8. NATO decisions on nuclear weapons are not debated in parliament.
9. Parliament is impotent due to lack of information, poor resources, and exclusion from the nuclear weapons policy process.
10. Decisions are taken by secret inner cabinet sub committees. The decision to buy Trident was taken by a group of five ministers. No discussion was held in the full cabinet, which was only told of the decision hours before it was announced in parliament.

[1] [Oxford Research Group, *Who Decides? Accountability and Nuclear Weapons Decision-Making in Britain*, ORG, 1986]

[2] [Hugh Miall, *Nuclear Weapons: Who's In Charge?* Macmillan, 1987]

is that? What you've described is another version of the disintegration thesis. The United States is in economic trouble with its big deficits etc, the UK is in a certain amount of trouble in terms of economic crisis, but what is the significance of this in terms of nuclear weapons? Are we arguing that whereas in the case of the Soviet Union we're knocking down the disintegration thesis as a basis for their use, in the case of the United States and the UK these irresponsible people might be prepared to nuke Baghdad, or wherever the next troublespot might be? Is that what we're saying?

Tony Carty: Yes. If nuclear weaponry or military hardware generally are to be a form of compensation for national insecurity in the face of economic competition, particularly from Japan, but also from Germany, then it may well be that the United States and the United Kingdom in tandem would search more and more for a military role and that there could be a drift away from the notion that weaponry should only be used in the context of the threat of annihilation to oneself. That is, I think, a danger.

Elizabeth Templeton: Well, that is what worries me and I also think that there's a kind of paradox because we're talking about what it is appropriate for reasonable people to believe. What you're describing as the threat internally in the American/British context, which I think is quite accurately described, is a kind of heading towards disaster, which is more liable to provoke irrational responses than rational ones. So it's a question of whether or not there's a way of putting some wedge in between public consciousness of what the actual situation is and the mythology of the power holders, who, one way or another, devise policy and manipulate opinion, because you've just said that the way decisions are taken about these matters are becoming less and less democratic, if they ever were democratic at all.

Malcolm Spaven: So we're getting into a situation, by your argument, and I go along with this, that Trident is actually increasingly irrelevant to the real conflicts. The problem is that it's forgotten about; it continues and it's forgotten about because people, perhaps rightly, concentrate on the more likely military conflicts and the use of conventional weaponry and the increasing likelihood of interventions like we've had in the Gulf War. Trident is wholly irrelevant in that sort of scenario. I want to develop that a little bit, because we talked earlier about whether Trident is still predicated solely on a *Soviet* threat, and broadly agreed that that was still the thrust of official policy. I'm not so sure about that. I think there are some shifts going on in official policy. If I could just quote Tom King, Secretary of State for Defence, in the debate in the House of Commons on the statement of the defence estimates last year, 18th June. He said, 'When one looks at the wider world one sees that the biggest problem at present, which no doubt worries the Soviet Union as well as the Western powers, is the degree of proliferation and the variety of missile and warhead capabilities. There is no doubt that we need to consider those aspects when looking at our defence plans'. Then Archie Hamilton, a Junior Defence Minister, the following day in the same debate said, 'The United Kingdom's strategic deterrent makes an important contribution to Alliance security and is the ultimate guarantee of our security and insurance policy against unwelcome developments in the future'. So, it seems to me that they're trying to make Trident fit the new scenario. Whether they succeed or not is another matter, but they're certainly trying and I think we need to address that.

Is Trident relevant to these new situations? The big thing that they always argue is, 'It's an uncertain world, particularly the growth of nuclear proliferation: this is something we really have to worry about'. So I think we have to address: first, does Trident actually deter nuclear proliferation? and second, does it deter the use of nuclear weapons once those countries have proliferated? You can point to the examples of near-nuclear states like Argentina and Iraq, which were prepared to go to war against nuclear states. Was British possession of nuclear weapons at all relevant to those situations? I think probably not.

You have also to come back to the point we mentioned earlier about the technical capability. If Trident is suddenly going to be switched from lobbing missiles at Moscow and penetrating all the anti-ballistic missile defences there, to deterring or threatening some other unknown country in the future, then the argument that Trident is a minimum deterrent collapses completely. Trident has to have lots of warheads in order to be sure at least one will get through the defences around Moscow. But there aren't any anti-ballistic missile defences anywhere else in the world. So you then have a massive system which, presumably, would be used to threaten some city or other, say, Buenos Aires or Baghdad. In that context, Trident is very definitely overkill. But we still have to ask, 'Is it technically feasible?' Do we have the maps and the data and the ability to re-target the missiles and the knowledge of the ocean areas where Trident would have to patrol in order to threaten those countries? And second, how would the country being threatened know it was being threatened, other than in a general sense that Britain has nuclear weapons? Certainly many people in the military would regard that as a crucial element of deterrence. You have to be able to get that information to your adversary, that you have this real capability, not in a general sense, but in an actual, specific, technical sense. I think that's a big problem. What do you do? Do you surface your Trident submarine, thereby giving its position away? Do you sail your submarine a few miles off Argentina to show that it's there? How do you do it? The Soviets know that they're being threatened all the time but would other countries be convinced if we said that they were?

Then you get beyond that and say, well, is it politically credible? That's where you get into the whole business of looking at the outcome of the Gulf War, and what has been happening to the feasibility of using military force in the world in the last ten years or so. There was a very interesting report in 1988 called *Discriminate Deterrence* which was written by a commission set up by Reagan to look at long-term US military strategy. One of the key things that it identified, right at the beginning of the report, was the fact that America can no longer regard itself as the economic superpower in the world and that there are many centres of economic power: Germany and Japan, yes, but South-East Asia as well. There are many developing countries there with major economic power which actually threaten the leadership of America in the world in many spheres. In that sort of situation, and with the collapse of the Soviet threat, nuclear deterrence is no longer as relevant and no longer as credible and the report comes out and says, 'Look, the one thing we're still quite good at is military technology in areas like Stealth, precision-guided weapons and the use of space for military purposes'. These were the three major military issues which came out of the Gulf War, in fact. So it's quite interesting to look at *Discriminate Deterrence* on the one hand and the Gulf War on the other. What it shows is that America is moving very steadily towards a policy of using deterrence in their terms 'more discriminately': in other words the more credible use of military force which is not massive nuclear retaliation.

The use of nuclear weapons is simply not credible in any conceivable scenario in the world now. If the real problem in the world is nuclear proliferation then the countries that feel the need to acquire nuclear weapons, you would argue, seem to see some benefit in having them. Whether that involves an intention to use them is maybe another matter, but then you have to ask, 'What is the solution to these countries acquiring nuclear weapons?' You could argue that the Gulf War was an example of non-proliferation in practice. If somebody has a near-nuclear capability you just send in a few conventional Cruise missiles and aircraft with smart weapons and you blow up their reactors. That's arguably a more feasible, less fraught and less lengthy way of achieving non-proliferation than going through the whole business of arms control and diplomatic negotiations.

Look at the Israelis: they were worried about Iraqi proliferation and what did they do? They sent in the F-16s and blew up the reactor. Ten years of Iraqi nuclear research out the window and that's much more credible. Okay, there was a certain degree of political fall-out from the Israelis doing that but they really haven't suffered, politically, in the world from having done that and I don't believe the Americans would either. So the whole conception of the use of military force is moving very much away from the basic idea of nuclear deterrence, which is you have these weapons in order not to use them; military force is becoming much more credible in its use now and that does put nuclear weapons in a very difficult position.

John Eldridge: Let's come back, then, to these arguments about the United States and the United Kingdom and the danger that they constitute to the world: apart from what you might call some loose talk, in terms of what Malcolm's just developed, from people like Vice-President Quayle, who said we might actually nuke Baghdad, what we're really saying is, 'That is a foolish, impractical rhetoric that was never really on'. But what is on is an approach towards the control of difficult regions which perhaps have some economic significance for industrial nations. A control based upon advanced technology, the use of very precise weapons and so on. Now, I suspect there might be a bit of rhetoric about that as well, but, nevertheless, the ideology of control through sophisticated weapons systems, rather than nuclear weapons—what this does is that it renders the traditional discussions and rationale for Cold War obsolete. But it raises quite new and important questions about the modes of international regulation. In other words, we're pointing to another kind of scenario which isn't particularly optimistic in terms of the militarisation of the world. It's just shifting the way in which it operates. That's something that we would need to address as well. In following our argument that Trident does indeed seem to be an obsolete system we now have another kind of argument to confront, which is a different form of militarisation, different form of control, given that we now have one world superpower, defined in military, not in economic terms.

David Pullinger: So we don't want to end up recommending a more and more effective military strategy, in other words?

John Eldridge: Well, we want to confront that as an issue, don't we?

Elizabeth Templeton: But confronting that is going to mean also that Tony's analysis is right. It's going to mean, in some way, the significant dismantling of capitalist assumptions, because what you've just been saying is that the state that capitalism has got itself into is one where it just cannot survive, except by this vast military complex as part of its structural skeleton. Now, if it's true that they stand or fall together in some way, it seems to me that the type of imagination needed has to move on to thinking about how a world handles itself, which clearly can't survive any longer in the Cold War, capitalism versus communism polarisation; but which recognises that this doesn't mean communism disintegrates and capitalism can somehow go on indefinitely under its own momentum, which is still the Western myth.

Tony Carty: Well, I think that underlying the notion of international law and non-proliferation of nuclear weapons is a basic moral point. It's also written into the Christian tradition, which is that we can't really expect other people not to acquire these weapons if we're not going to discard them eventually. So built in to the non-proliferation treaty arrangement is the understanding that those countries already in possession of weapons are actually going to disarm. Now, that brings me on immediately to what I think is the fundamental moral, cultural and spiritual flaw in the Anglo-American notion of the policeman, which is basically that evil is always outside. There's never any question of interrogating one's own house. Somehow or other by some miraculous historical process the United States has been given, presumably by God, responsibility for ensuring that the entire universe conducts itself in a proper manner, and this is the unquestioned assumption that underlies the whole notion of the new international order.

I think that, in institutional terms—that's not talking about political practicalities—the way to turn this round is that the United Nations' role as a peacekeeping force should be fully implemented in terms of having an international police force actually under the authority of the Security Council. Then if police actions were necessary they would be undertaken by a UN multilateral military force and not by some kind of unilateral commander, rather as you had with the Gulf crisis, where the United Nations rubber-stamped American initiatives. There's a very strong feeling, even among conservative elements, that one should strengthen the United Nations as a multilateral force to get away from this unilateralist United States moral tradition. Now, I think this American mentality to which Britain then says, 'Yes' and 'Amen' is rooted in a particular Puritan, Christian notion of the nature of society and the nature of order and the nature of evil. Basically, the righteous have to inherit, or have already inherited, the Earth. I think one has to take seriously here, and not simply indulge in cheap anti-Americanism, the fact that for example Bush himself, as far as we can see, has presented his own decision-making process in the context of the Gulf in religious terms: he went on retreat prayer sessions and reflection and decided what he felt God required of him in this context. This has to be taken at face value as very serious.

Elizabeth Templeton: Well, I think it has to be taken seriously, but I think also that it becomes less and less plausible if you look at the self-description in global terms, because the documentation is massing all the time for what mishandling of the world we've done from our Western base. So more and more strain can be put on this as a credible self-description. I think it may well be the case that, subjectively, Bush and right-wing Americans or Europeans still 'innocently' believe they are God's gift to the world; but from the rest of the world's point of view it's nonsense. I think this can be clearly documented when you look at the impact of the whole Western economic machine on the Third World, for example.

Tony Carty: As for the internal critique then—here I'm talking in terms of the influence of religion on political culture—I think there are two elements of the Puritan tradition which are menacing. First, there is its righteousness, when this reproduces itself in any fundamentalist tradition, and the United States is more and more likely to be confronted, and is being confronted, by an Islamic version of the same thing. Second, the craving for security that this religious fanaticism represents is closely related to the whole military security question. I think there's probably a connection between the worst case scenario mentality of the American military establishment and this fundamentalist religious tradition. You think of the regiments going off to the Gulf:

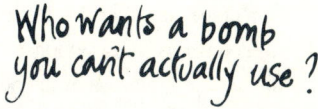

Who wants a bomb you can't actually use?

SCRAP TRIDENT

as they were portrayed on American TV, they went off singing hymns using Old Testament imagery. But is Trident relevant even in relation to its strong craving for security? The difficulty is that one can go beyond the development of an effective military force for a policing role on the international scene to becoming a threat and a menace.

John Eldridge: Can we think a bit more about this? The notion of the armies of the righteous, as it were. Presumably you could go back to a whole set of Old Testament documentation about being on the right side and the 'Lord of hosts is with us'— this sense of the God of battles. Then you see that appropriated, say, in Cromwell's armies. Again, this notion of a sword and the Cross and the Bible coming together in this sense of crusading righteousness. In the case of the United States it seems to me that if you want to pursue this argument, I would see it reflected in their doctrine of manifest destiny. This particularly had reference to the Central American and Latin American states where, if things were out of order, you sent the US troops in to get them in order. The whole business of the banana republics was that what America did in its back yard was justified. We can understand there were economic reasons, in terms of a certain notion of sustaining the civilising process, extending the democratic process and so on. America was the great democratic expression of the New World—this new world, this new force, this new righteousness being demonstrated. And then, very importantly, the anti-communism of the post-war period which was manifested both within the United States and, of course, in terms of its foreign policy. So that anti-communism was really a crusade against evil—there was never any doubt about this.

It seems to me that that kind of rhetoric can be used for various purposes, whatever your particular arena of conflict. It can be used in Vietnam, but it can also be used, as we saw, in the case of the Gulf. So you then introduce the rhetoric of the just war in order to defeat demonic powers, this time represented in

Saddam Hussein. There's a lot of very strong ideological material there which can be used, and in fact is culturally embedded in the minds of the political leaders and many people in that country. But then you have to set that alongside the sheer cynicism, brutality and opportunism of the practice whereby you go round and you sew up deals with Egypt, with Saudi Arabia, with Syria, who just previously had been the enemy. You sew up deals with them and in the name of the 'just war' you then wage war to liberate Kuwait. Meanwhile, you perhaps encourage the Kurds to rise in Iraq, but when it comes to it you're not really in the business of supporting the Kurds because there are reasons of international power play that mean you're not going to do that. In other words, alongside this incredible righteous, crusading attitude to the whole business of what we are here for as a nation, the American nation, we have these incredibly cynical power politics which will simply sell the Kurds down the river, as they did in the 1970s and as they're doing now. Doesn't that lead us to reflect upon the authenticity of that kind of religious vision?

Elizabeth Templeton: It's also such a selective religious vision, even in its own terms. What I think must be argued is that side by side, both in the Old Testament and in the New Testament, you've got two really quite incompatible visions of security in relation to God. One of them is the kind of Wells Fargo view: right, you just walk across this river and I'll deal with the blokes who are already on the other side and we'll bash all these Hephites and Hittites and you can have the land because I'm your good guy, God. But at the same time running through a lot of the Isaiah stuff, for example, and certainly centrally through the way the

Cross theme's understood in the New Testament, you've got the view that it is almost the opposite: that what you can afford to do, because you are secure in God, is offer no resistance. Let your security actually depend on something that you don't carry in your own hands, and so you're able to be far more vulnerable than you would be in the other line.

Tony Carty: My understanding of it is basically that you don't need to have a worst case scenario for the future, but that what will happen is what should happen. I think there's a certain passivity in relation to it. I also think that, while I make these bitter criticisms of the Americans, part of the Christian tradition is very much that we are all part of another, whatever it is we're talking about or thinking about, and there is a danger of demonising the American political establishment ourselves. I came across a few weeks ago something I had looked up a long time ago in connection with the Vietnam War, a very remarkable and lucid statement by Senator Fulbright who was Chairman of the Senate Foreign Relations Committee at that time. He wrote a book called *The Arrogance of Power* in which he studied the American religious tradition in the context of foreign affairs, and traced the policeman role to Theodore Roosevelt, in the early twentieth century. But, while on the one hand there is the policeman function that we have been criticising, there is another American tradition which he thinks, perhaps questionably, is represented by Abraham Lincoln. He quotes Abraham Lincoln as saying, 'There are many, many things which many men do which I find remarkable, but then as Scriptures said, "Let us not judge for as we judge so shall we be judged".' So there has been, in the kind of early youth of the American Republic, very much a feeling of resistance to the European concert system and the behaviour of European powers; a feeling that American destiny is to put one's own house in order, to look after one's own affairs and not to have opinions about how everyone else should get on with their affairs. Now this is

Christian Accounts of Security

From the Hebrew Scriptures, Christianity inherits two accounts of 'security' which seem hard to reconcile.

1. God makes his people secure by defeating their enemies, giving their land into his people's power, making supernatural interventions on their behalf, offering special protections, e.g. the Passover escape from Egypt; the Joshua story. [The living God is among you, and he will without fail drive out from before the Canaanites, the Hittites, the Hivites, the Perizzites, the Girgashites, the Amorites and the Jebusites] Joshua 3:10
2. God gives his chosen ones the security to suffer without retaliation, knowing that their vindication rests with God alone, e.g. the Suffering Servant theme in Isaiah 53, and insists on the forgiveness of enemies, even at the cost of the forgiver's pain.

The New Testament maintains both perspectives. The basic perspective of Acts, for example, is triumphalist and celebrates a God who eliminates the opposition for his people. This is hard to reconcile with the tradition that presents Jesus as commanding love of enemies, turning the other cheek, etc, and with the central Passion narrative.

The history of Christendom presents similarly diverse models.

On one hand, there are the martyr tradition (sometimes involving whole communities), the strong 'Theology of the Cross' theme, the pacifist minorities (Quaker, Mennonite, etc). On the other, there is the dominant tendency since Church and state fused after Constantine, for secular armies to have been seen as supported by God as collaborators in providing security for 'his' people. Hence the blessing of battleships, bombs, etc.

a sentiment that dictated most of American foreign policy from the time of independence until Theodore Roosevelt, at the beginning of the twentieth century. A significant foreign policy initiative had been to kick the French out of Mexico, but that was the implementing of a non-interventionist policy.

I think what we could want to encourage or want to consider is a less negative view of isolationism on the part of the United States. How could the United States be encouraged to go back to this 'one nation among nations' attitude towards its role in international affairs? That is deeply rooted in American culture, as well, in earlier times and was reflected in American policy in the inter-war period. The anxiety about the consequences of the policy is played out in the language of responsibility, the threat of Nazi-type forces to world order and the consequences of American isolationism. But I think Fulbright's paradigms, even within a religious context, in American political culture are there. These two tendencies may well be working within Bush himself, because on the one hand he has this righteous determination to purge the sin of Iraq in invading Kuwait and on the other hand he has this very strong feeling that he doesn't really understand very much about what makes the Middle East tick and so he doesn't want to have to involve American troops permanently in sorting out Iraq's problems because that's beyond his capacity. So, taking a slightly more optimistic view, I think it may be possible to work within these traditions, to point to a kind of spiritual modesty which doesn't show itself very often.

John Eldridge: Elizabeth's view about the security débâcle makes me think a little mischievously about the Isaac Watts hymn which is sung at the Cenotaph: 'Oh God, our help in Ages Past'. There's that line, 'Sufficient is thine arm alone and our defence is sure'. It refers to God's arm, not to our arm, obviously. It's slightly curious when people sing this in full dress uniform ...

I would like to ask a question about the way this nuclear deterrence issue emerged in discussion and in practical relations with the United States. It seems to me that if you go back to the Second World War you have a close Anglo-American relationship which leads to the building of the atom bomb. You then have the post-war situation where on the one hand the United States has its bases in Britain and elsewhere in Europe as part of the Cold War posture, and on the other hand Britain is trying to

> The American academic, Ullman, learned through unattributable interviews with over 100 senior officials in the US and France, that the US assistance to the French nuclear weapons programme began in 1973, under the Nixon administration. Initially restricted to non-nuclear assistance, for example, on missile development or the state of Soviet ABM defences, the programme grew to encompass miniaturisation and electromagnetic shielding of warheads, safety and security technology, and use of the Nevada test site. The principal rationale for the co-operation, Ullman found, was a US desire to coax France back into the political mainstream, and to undo some of the damage to US-French relations under de Gaulle. US military planners have also been keen to encourage better co-ordination of nuclear forces within NATO; not knowing where French missiles were targeted was always a severe drawback.
>
> [Richard K Ullman, 'The Covert French Connection', *Foreign Policy*, No. 75, Summer 1989, p 3-33]

keep in the atom club. There is an argument (here I'm following David Leigh's exposition) which suggests that while the Anglo-American relationship was quite strong there was also an element of mismatch or even mistrust about it because the Americans did not want the British to have an independent nuclear deterrent. It was Bevin and Attlee, in the first Labour government, in very secret circumstances which actually excluded members of their own cabinet, who encouraged and made possible the development of Britain's own atomic bomb. This then became the basis of our independent nuclear deterrent. That is followed through across the political parties, but at the same time the nature of that independence is eroded, almost from the word go, because we did become dependent upon the Americans for technology and servicing.

But the paradox, to me anyway, is that what the concern for independence really amounts to and, in a curious way, is built upon, is some mistrust of the Americans. For that matter, the Americans had some mistrust of us because they didn't want us to have the deterrent. I don't know whether that's a particular reading of the history which other people wouldn't agree with, but if it's anywhere near the mark then it does remind us of a very curious origin of our own history in terms of our participation in the nuclear club. Forty years on, or whatever it is, I think perhaps we need to look at that again and say, if that's the origin, do we have to live with that kind of history?

Malcolm Spaven: Yes. It seems to me that, from the start, Britain wanted to think of itself as operating on equal terms with the Americans in terms of nuclear capability, or as far as possible, equal terms. There has always been this mistrust on the part of the Americans of British motives. At the same time, the British have wanted to be able to say that their deterrent is independent, but there are so many examples of Britain having to go back and beg to the Americans because they're technically not capable of doing the task on their own. That was more or less sealed right from the start by the fact that the Americans cut off the supply of information after the Quebec Agreement in 1943.

Tony Carty: The British always complained about it; at the same time as they were wanting to exclude the French from any kind of—

Malcolm Spaven: This is an interesting point that is probably quite relevant. There's some evidence come out recently from an American academic, Ullman, who interviewed key French and US officials involved with nuclear weapons. He has discovered that there's a long history of French secret co-operation with the Americans on their nuclear weapons. And yet all this debate about 'independence—or not' simply does not happen in France. Maybe it's because they're more successful about keeping it quiet or maybe it's just that it's seen as being a necessary technical arrangement which you don't have to worry about because France is not giving up any of its political inde-

The Quebec Agreement

From the early stages of Britain's nuclear weapons research in 1941-42, scientific co-operation with the US developed rapidly. But the Americans became suspicious that British scientists had nothing tangible to offer and co-operation was merely to develop a nuclear programme of their own. The Americans stopped supplying information in 1943.

Churchill and Roosevelt then initiated direct talks culminating in the Quebec Agreement, which was signed with the Canadians on 19 August 1943. The key element was that the US and Britain agreed never to use an atomic bomb against any third party without the other's consent. In addition, it re-established scientific exchange between the three parties.

After the war, the US again began to limit British access to information. Prime Minister Attlee wrote several pleading letters to Truman during 1946, but in the meantime the US Congress passed the MacMahon Act, making it illegal for any US government employee to pass nuclear information to another state. This led directly to the British government decision in January 1947 to develop its own atom bomb.

Britain also abandoned its veto over US use of the bomb. After Hiroshima and Nagasaki, a watered-down version of the Quebec Agreement had been drafted, which allowed for use of the bomb with prior 'consultation', rather than consent, of the other parties, while pledging to 'prevent the use of atomic energy for destructive purposes'. That draft was never adopted, but in January 1948, a new agreement called the 'Modus Vivendi' was signed, in which the British government abandoned the right of veto over US use of the bomb entirely, apparently trying to maintain the flow of information from the US bomb programme.

A thaw in Anglo-US nuclear relations developed, and in 1951 the MacMahon Act was amended, allowing information exchange to resume. After Britain exploded its first bomb in 1952, the US authorities believed the best way to prevent full-scale weapons production was to allow greater access to information, and to link this with agreements to deploy US nuclear bombers to Britain in times of crisis. The strategy clearly did not work, but it set the stage for the 1958 Agreement for Co-operation on the Uses of Atomic Energy for Mutual Defence Purposes, which formed the basis of the extensive Anglo-US nuclear collaboration which continues today.

pendence. The French are not selling their security, but simply getting hold of particular bits of technology which will benefit France. Perhaps the difference is that in Britain we have had several cases where the Americans have turned round and abrogated deals that people are relying on, e.g. the Quebec Agreement in 1943. Then you had the decision to buy Skybolt missiles in the late 1950s, early 1960s, and then the Americans turned round and cancelled Skybolt. We gave up our missile capability as a result and eventually bought Polaris, to which Kennedy said, 'Well, you can only have Polaris if you assign them to NATO; we're not having you as a totally national nuclear capability'.

So perhaps the difference between Britain and France is that dependence on the Americans in these several cases where we've been faced with an American *fait accompli*. The same, of course, applies with Trident. I'm sure lots of people in the British establishment didn't really want Trident. They wanted something technically sensible to replace Polaris but they didn't really want the escalation that was inevitable with Trident. I suppose that you could argue that Trident One was a rather more sensible replacement but a year later the Americans came along and said, 'Well, actually, we're going to get rid of Trident One and have Trident Two instead. It's a much bigger missile, longer range etc,' and the British just had to go along with that. So in that sense we've been very dependent on American decisions which we have no influence over.

John Eldridge: Could it be that the difference between us and the French is that the French relation to NATO is rather different and therefore they can speak about their *force de frappe* and so on as something which is theirs? They don't need to make a big production of the fact that it's independent in quite that linguistic way. Whereas, in the British case, if we are part of NATO in a more integrated way then we have to stress the independence. My own view about that is that it harmonises very well with our history and our sense of ourselves as an important

British Reliance on Nuclear Decisions

YEAR	US	BRITAIN
1946	Congress passes the MacMahon Act; nuclear information stops	
1947		Britain decides to build its own bomb.
1948		Britain abandons veto over US use of atomic weapons, permits US bombers to be based in Britain.
1952		First British atom bomb test; operational A-bombs not in RAF service until 1956.
1957	First H-bombs enter service with USAF	
1958	Treaty on Use of Atomic Energy for Mutual Defence Purposes signed; allows for transfer of bomb assemblies and fissile materials to Britain, to make copies of US bomb designs.	
1960		US bombs supplied to RAF V-bomber force to compensate for delays in British H-bomb development.
1960	US agrees to supply Skybolt missiles for RAF V-bombers in exchange for access to Holy Loch submarines.	Blue Streak missile programme cancelled - UK ballistic missile capability abandoned for good.
1961		First British copies of US bomb designs enter service with RAF.
1962	US cancels Skybolt, but agrees to supply Polaris missiles for a nuclear missile submarine force.	
1967		Labour government approves research into new warhead for Polaris. By early 1970s programme runs into difficulties. US help sought.
1973	President Nixon refuses Heath government request to buy Poseidon missiles.	

world leader, that is the leaders of an empire, now the leaders of the Commonwealth and significant actors on the world stage. Such significance needs to be accompanied by the appropriate nuclear weapons, which would lead even Bevan, in that famous statement, to say that he didn't want to go naked into the conference chamber, which assumes that it's worth going into the conference chamber in the first place.

Malcolm Spaven: But the interesting thing there is that the Americans seem to have had less mistrust of France than they had of Britain. They insisted that Britain allocate Polaris submarines to NATO; they've been very careful about what, exactly, they've given to Britain in the way of technology and so on; and yet the French, who kicked all American bases out in 1966 and left the military structure of NATO have subsequently been getting this nuclear co-operation from America.

John Eldridge: That's a very pragmatic question. If the grounding is on a sort of mutual mistrust and now we know that Trident is dependent, heavily, upon American service, why should we be very confident about the future in terms of America's own defence needs, defence strategies and policies about its own issues? Why should we feel very confident that it will continue to supply us with what we want?

Malcolm Spaven: I think that's right. I think that history shows that Britain has been the victim of all kinds of American decisions where they've made shifts in their strategy or their procurement. I think we are now reaching another of those situations where the Americans are reorganising their forces very radically; they're thinking about the changing role of strategic weapons

Reliance on Nuclear Decisions (cont'd)

YEAR	US	BRITAIN
1974	US cancels Antelope project on which new UK warhead was based.	UK government approves go-it-alone Chevaline programme. Six years and £1,000 million later, the project is revealed to parliament.
1977		Labour government considers options for replacing Polaris.
1978	President Carter tells Prime Minister Callaghan that USA is prepared to supply Trident.	
1979	Trident I (C4) enters service with US Navy.	
1980		Britain announces purchase of Trident I (C4) to replace Polaris.
1981	US announces phasing out of Trident I, replacement by 'hard target' and longer-range Trident II (D5).	
1982		Britain switches to Trident II. Britain to lease missiles from US pool rather than purchasing own sole-use inventory; servicing to be carried out in US rather than Coulport.

in the world, unlike the British government; and they're talking about achieving a kind of unified strategic force as opposed to having three separate service organisations that are always fighting each other. One of the main reasons why America has so many strategic weapons of different kinds is because you have some in the navy and some in the air force and, even within the air force you have bombers and missiles, and the different communities are always fighting each other for procurement funds and for particular bits of technology that they want to pursue. The result is basically that they end up with all of them. But now there does seem to be some serious discussion in the States about trying to remove some of those competitive pressures and to create a rather more integrated strategy and, who knows, that might result in submarine launched ballistic missiles becoming much less important. The British may end up with the same situation that they had in the late 1960s when the Americans closed down Polaris production. They didn't have Polaris any more and we ended up having to service a missile that was no longer in production, the spares were in decline and so on.

David Pullinger: Can I ask a small technical question? In the midst of this you described Britain as not being technically able to build an independent nuclear weapons facility. To what extent is that a technical problem or a resource problem?

Malcolm Spaven: I think it's mainly a technical question because if you look at the Chevaline programme, for example, a project that started in the early 1970s, it was, as most British nuclear weapons have been, an American design which was then adapted in order to incorporate a slightly different configuration of the nuclear material inside it. In the case of many of these weapons it's simply that the Americans provided the blueprints—even provided dummy weapons without nuclear material in them, the actual physical product—and the British tried to copy it. If you look at the Chevaline programme, they tried to do that sort of thing in order to put a new warhead on Polaris; the Americans cancelled their end of the programme for their own missiles in 1974 and the British ended up trying to go it alone. They spent over £1 billion and we eventually got there, but only after spending huge amounts of money with reference to no one else and with little or no American support. If you go back to the

The Escalation from Polaris to Trident II

POLARIS	UK TRIDENT II (D5)

Submarines:
4 Resolution Class	4 Vanguard Class
(8,4000 tons displacement)	(15,000 tons displacement)

Missiles (16 per submarine):
Length: 31 ft 6 in	44 ft
Launch weight: 35,000 lb	130,000 lb
Range: 2,500 nautical miles	Up to 6,000 nautical miles
Accuracy: approx 1,000 yd CEP[1]	Probably 400-500 yd CEP[1]

Warheads:
Chevaline (UK designed and built)	Apparently a British adaptation of the US W-76, on the Mk.4 re-entry vehicle originally designed for Trident I.
Multiple re-entry vehicles, but not independently targetable	Multiple independently-targetable re-entry vehicles
2 - 3 warheads per missile	Up to 8 warheads per missile[2]
Yield: 40-50 kilotons each	US original is 1000 kilotons

[1] CEP (Circular Error Probable): the radius of a circle around the target within which 50% of warheads would be expected to fall.
[2] The British government has stated that it will not deploy more than 128 warheads per Trident submarine.

[Statement on the Defence Estimates 1987, p 41]

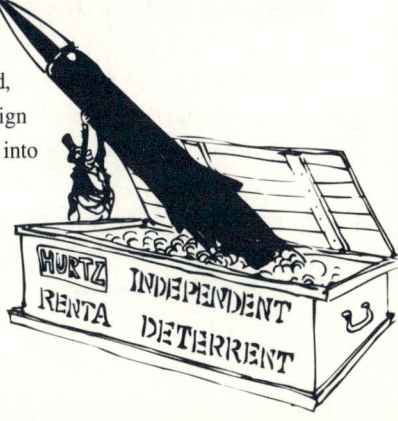

1950s, the early British bombs were, apparently, more or less British designed, with a lot of American design assistance, but then we ran into problems with not being able to support those, not having the capacity to support further research and we ended up, again, simply buying American weapons. There's some evidence which has come out in the last few years that even the supposedly completely independent V-bomber force actually had American nuclear weapons on the airfield, guarded by American security police and this was a stop-gap measure because we were unable to build the bombs ourselves. The evidence is that, even with substantially greater resources, Britain would have had a lot of difficulty in completely doing it on its own.

Tony Carty: There's a twist to this technological dependency argument that has come up in a book by the President of the Japanese Liberal Party, Shintaro Ishihara, which alleges that the whole Soviet/American détente and dismantling of military weaponry is attributable to the fact that the Pentagon itself now realises that its own weapons systems are dependent upon Japanese semi-conductors and technology and that, in fact, the US is upstaged, no longer being the leading technological power in the world. This is one more example of a radical destructuring of the stable international paradigms with which Britain worked for a long time, thinking that it could easily attach itself to the major, or decisive, world power, but now inevitably it will have to adjust to the fact that it's very difficult to trace where that major power is. The Japanese relationship with the US is unstable. It continues to supply this technology but it's not certain to do so in the future. The line that Ishihara is taking is that it's time for Japan to take up some kind of political role in the world and to translate its economic power into political power.

A second unrelated point which I find fascinating is that the military notion of oneself as a great power is decadent. The idea that you are a great power because you have certain squibs and nuts and bolts is pathetic if you look at the way that Britain constructed its power in the past. Imperial power in the good old days was based figuratively on rape and murder, plunder and pillage. That is to say power is not about status symbols, it's about realistic brute force. Power, nowadays, is about having the massive economic, industrial, technological infrastructure to support weaponry. It's quite clear Britain doesn't have that and it's equally clear to the Soviets, especially after the Gulf War, but even before, as we can see on the détente front. So the clinging to weapons, to the fact that one can purchase weapons as an indication of one's significance has to be analysed in terms of a deep decay of the British nation's political culture. I can't imagine Cromwell trying to buy some kind of cannon from Louis XIV in order to kid himself that Britain was a major power!

Malcolm Spaven: Isn't it simply that it dents Britain's pride to have to admit that it is so totally dependent on somebody else for its weapons? The other side of the Japan argument is that the Japanese have been buying American weapons for a large number of years, and does it actually matter in terms of your ability to protect yourself? Does it undermine your image? As a military power, does it matter that your missiles are full of Japanese microchips?

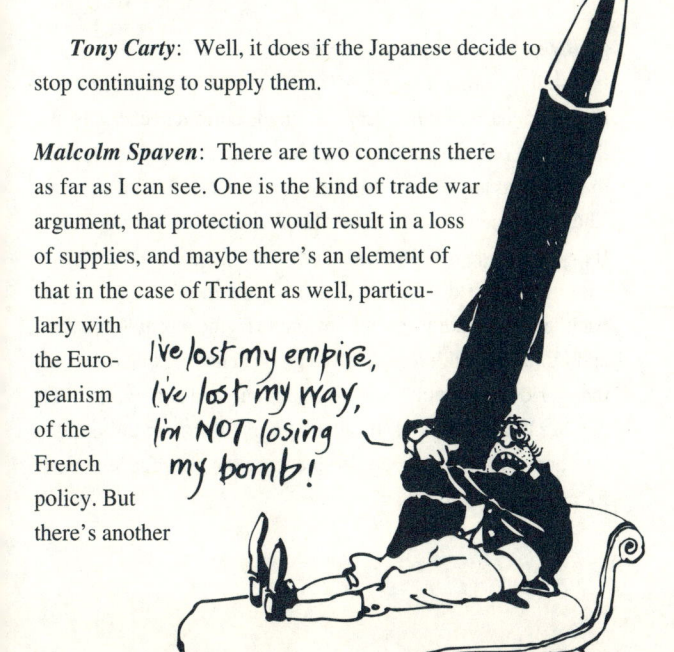

Tony Carty: Well, it does if the Japanese decide to stop continuing to supply them.

Malcolm Spaven: There are two concerns there as far as I can see. One is the kind of trade war argument, that protection would result in a loss of supplies, and maybe there's an element of that in the case of Trident as well, particularly with the Europeanism of the French policy. But there's another

I've lost my empire, I've lost my way, I'm NOT losing my bomb!

aspect to this which is that so-called strategic industries have to be protected and that you're not a proper military or economic power unless you have those strategic industries yourself. Now it seems to me that that argument basically goes back to the Second World War: all the thinking is that strategic industries are necessary because the sort of war that you're planning to fight is going to last five or six years. Therefore you have to have that production capability yourself because you cannot rely on trade. Frankly, that is nonsense now. Even before the disintegration of the Soviet Union, if you believe nuclear deterrence, if there had been a war in Europe there would probably have been a nuclear conflagration. Then the whole thing would have been over very quickly and strategic industries wouldn't have mattered one way or the other. Nowadays we're into a situation where the wars that are likely to take place are more likely to be like the Gulf War. They'll last a few weeks, they might be quite destructive, at least on one side, they might destroy somebody's strategic industries, but they certainly won't threaten the strategic industries of Britain or America.

Elizabeth Templeton: Well, I don't know if that's true indefinitely either. It seems to me that one of the lessons we're having to learn, and not very fast, in the current decades, is that the notion of independence is a kind of myth and that anything that happens anywhere in the world touches all the other points. There's something in Chaos Theory, which is, 'If a butterfly flaps its wings in Tokyo then something happens on the other side of the world'. That's clearly documented already, years back, in the Brandt Report for example on the North/South axis, and I think we can't let ourselves go on believing that one bit of the world can remain intact and immune and safe while other bits are being wrecked. It's that new mentality of unbounded interdependence that seems to me to be the only feasible basis for any political future.

Tony Carty: I think what you and Malcolm are saying together means that in terms of industrial technology it doesn't make any sense any longer to think of individual nations having a military apparatus that can protect their independence.

Elizabeth Templeton: I think that's just what I'm saying.

Tony Carty: At the same time I think there is something badly wrong with that. You go from the devil to the deep blue sea. It's true that we're all interdependent at every level but that still doesn't mean that we are not all autonomous at the same time. The peculiar difficulty for the UK, and other European countries to a lesser extent, is this dependence on the US which is an extremely complex matter that we haven't really broached very much. Barnett, in his books about the collapse of British power in the aftermath of the war, tries to analyse the philosophical reasons for this collapse. When was the point at which Britain ceased to act in a realistic Machiavellian view of what its own power interests were and started to adopt a fetishising of an equality with the Americans based on what weaponry they had? In the 1920s it was the size of the naval fleets and so on. How could one encourage the development of a genuinely bullish British foreign policy that was rooted in some kind of independent conception of what national interest was? That is a precondition of an interdependent system in which each individual unit has some sense of autonomy.

Elizabeth Templeton: I certainly don't think the alternative is a kind of national collectivism or this kind of very individualistic national identity being defended at all cost. But I do think interdependence is something which is really breaking down these poles of individualism on the one hand, collectivism on the other, because each unit—however the unit's arrived at —has its own contribution to make to the future, quite irreplaceably. If you start knocking any of them out then you're moving in the direction of some kind of totalitarianism, I suppose.

John Eldridge: Are we touching on something here where the notion of the independent nuclear deterrent is just one manifestation of a more general thing? The linguistic contrasts between independence and dependence, historically the freeborn Englishman and all that, the notion that independence and freedom are things that go together. Dependence implies some notion of subservience. Now that contrast between independence and dependence is something which I've certainly noticed over the last ten years in terms of new-right philosophy which is all about the importance of independence, the importance of standing on our own two feet, and what a dreadful thing it is to be dependent upon others. Therefore we talk about healthy independent and unhealthy dependent cultures. In other words that contrast is embedded, it seems to me, in the way in which we speak about our culture, certainly on the right. If you introduce the notion of interdependence as something that you have to work through in pluralist terms, it then becomes much more subtle. You begin to ask yourself what it is that is implied in notions of interdependence, whether we're talking about welfare or international relations or whatever. You don't abolish power because interdependence still implies some sort of power relationship. It's not the plurality of equals all the time. Yet once we allow that concept into the discussion we are breaking the dichotomy and we're perhaps saying something about the type of world we live in. So, to go back to the notion of independent nuclear deterrence, it seems to me that we can understand how such a concept comes into play, but perhaps it is actually an archaic concept which doesn't address realities.

Ian Kellas: One strand of the concept is that the nuclear capability is meant to be independent and it's meant to be a deterrent but no longer has any political impact beyond our own myth-making about ourselves. But can we dismiss it that easily? I always had this idea that it was supposed to be useful because if you didn't have it then you were going to be open to blackmail from whoever else did have it. They wouldn't actually have to spell out how they would use it—it was just enough to know that they had that ability to incinerate you and then you would be much more inclined to make serious, political compromises.

Tony Carty: The Barnett and Chomsky interpretation of British/American history is that that is precisely what has happened in the relationship between the UK and the US through the two world wars. In return for military assistance from the US Britain handed over to America vast amounts of foreign assets and resources and paved the way for the break up of the empire after the war, which the Americans regarded as very much an opportunity of attaining their own economic interests; for example forcing Commonwealth preferences in a new multinational trading system like GATT. We've been pretty sentimental about it but the Americans have really walked Britain to the bank over this.

John Eldridge: I'd like to get back to Ian's point because the notion of blackmail is certainly—

Tony Carty: That's certainly what's happened to Britain.

John Eldridge: But that wasn't nuclear. You see, this is the question. It seems to me that if that argument stands it stands for any non-nuclear power and that is the argument for proliferation, that nobody can be blackmailed if they have nuclear weapons. The question arises whether people are blackmailed by the fact that, say, the US has nuclear weapons or whether the kind of control which a superpower like the US can say it's going to operate is based on quite other considerations, maybe other kinds of weaponry. I think the Gulf War reminds us that quite other things are happening. What we have had since the Second

World War is a large number of wars outwith the European arena which have been non-nuclear wars. Therefore the question of nuclear blackmail has not stopped wars happening. But it remains the case that a superpower like the US is still able to achieve great things, not because it's a nuclear power but because of other considerations.

Ian Kellas: Because it's a conventional superpower as well.

John Eldridge: Yes, all the economic pressure that it's able to operate and geopolitical considerations.

Tony Carty: Because it's following your réalpolitik. While Britain has had a moral role for itself in the world since the Second World War, America has been dominated by realist theories of international society. Morganthau et al as leading international specialists in the US only very recently have come to look for a place for morality in American theories of international society. Realist theory is under very severe attack.

John Eldridge: So that real power in international relations, in the end, has not been dependent upon nuclear weapons.

Ian Kellas: So what is the function of nuclear weapons for the Americans? Is it to use the arms race to bankrupt the Soviet Union? In which case they've been rather successful.

Tony Carty: I think that is one policy that they seem to have executed very successfully. I remember, when we were going through our previous circle of discussions, thinking I had discovered something very shocking and radical. I found the Pentagon Report to Congress of 1981 in which Defence Secretary Weinberger reported, 'The object of our defence build-up and strategy is to bust the Soviet economy', which they seem to have done successfully. That's what I mean by réalpolitik. I've always been struck by Weinberger as such a down-to-earth, ordinary kind of person who is not interested in grand theories but just this realistic cynical analysis of society. Once again, I stress that the country that's walked into blackmail in international relations is Britain in its relations with America, taking what it's given up in order to have this close military collaboration with the Americans.

John Eldridge: The point I'm making is—blackmail is not because America was a nuclear power.

Tony Carty: Oh, definitely I agree with you there.

John Eldridge: It was for quite other reasons, and certain people go through—

Tony Carty: Well, it's in a sense that America's a nuclear power and Britain wants to be—that's the sense. But it's a very ironical twist.

John Eldridge: So our involvement, our 'neutrality' in relation to the Vietnam War and things of that sort were things which the Americans bought. So a Labour government which you might have expected to oppose the Vietnam War actually kept quiet.

Ian Kellas: The whole drift of this argument is that Britain, with these silly notions of imperial grandeur, has just made a fool of itself in international affairs. But it seems to me that you could argue the opposite: that we are basically an insignificant world power now and yet we do have quite high status, because of our military prestige, and because we have been hanging on to Uncle Sam's coat tails. And he is still, basically, running the show. We may not be able to go on doing it very much longer, but it has worked so far.

Malcolm Spaven: I think that's the temptation. I think that's the allure that the US continues to present to Britain. Britain is a competent military power: it beat the Argentinians and got back the Falklands and the operation there got quite a reputation. And it has competent insurgency operations in Northern Ireland. As a military force the army seems to run rather better than a lot of industry. But I think that comes back to the pride in the armed forces as a symbol of national identity.

Elizabeth Templeton: I'm still fascinated by this question of identity and what shifts are taking place, or are going to have to take place, and how we understand our identity. I think the national self-understandings are very much macrocosms of different ways that people understand themselves and I think the British or the British/American pole has been very much that you start with the individual, the atomic reality, who then has various options relating here or there. But basically you are most yourself by yourself and then you move into optional relationships. Now, I think there's another view of identity which I would say is a collectivist one in which you are just a cog in the wheel and therefore, in a sense, you're dispensable. Or at least you are only valuable and important as you function in the whole set-up.

I think myself that one of the contributions, theologically, that has to be made to the understanding of what it is to be a person is that Christian thinking rejects both of these and says you are not most really you as an individual and you are not most really you as a part of a collective whole. You are most really you as someone in relation and to be a person is essentially to be someone in relation, someone to whom someone else is irreplaceable and who is irreplaceable to someone else so that there is mutuality built into your very sense of your identity. Now, I think if that were to be recovered, not necessarily in terms of Christian dogma, but in terms of human self-understanding, either at the personal level or at the national/international level, you would have a much more creative base for international relationships, as well as for personal ones.

I don't know Russian at all, but I think the idea that Russian theologians make of *Sobornost* is really something to do with that. It's to know that you are only strong as you relate to the other. I think that that is almost becoming the lesson of history and becoming palpable to more and more people. That you can't survive as an atom, you can't survive as part of a collective, that there has to be some open relating in which you say to one another, 'I need you to know who I am'.

Tony Carty: What now occurs to me is an alternative model of international society, not one in which the British have to choose between total dependence on the Americans or absorption in the European Community or getting back to the Cromwellian island race, but one in which each nation has an immensely varied, complex relationship with lots of different peoples. There's no reason why Britain shouldn't play the function *within* the European Community of insisting on the Atlantic dimension, of the immense complexity of interdependent personal relations which should take place at all levels. That should be the model for the future as against the power bloc model of the past. A lot of the talk on the Continent at the moment is about trying to replace the Soviet power bloc as a balancing force against America with a European power bloc. But that's a trap, that's collectivist thinking losing itself in a European collectivity. My ideal of international law opposes this. The system of international law we have at present is basically concerned with delineating the autonomy and competences of the different state jurisdictions.

The way I want to teach international law is to study the concrete bilateral relations which actually grow up between all the different communities on the Earth so that these bilateral relationships are seen to be constantly interacting and criss-crossing. Britain may have relations with the Americans about some things, with the Soviets about others, with the Germans about others again etc. You have a *web* of different kinds of contacts going in different directions. All these affirm their identity in relationship instead of affirming identity in separation, which is—

Elizabeth Templeton: I think the web image is a very important one in all kinds of context.

Tony Carty: The web is not sufficient because we find ourselves facing the dilemma that in fact we start to form clubs, like the EC and then suddenly our old relationships with the Commonwealth are threatened. We can't live within static webs of bilateral agreements all the time.

John Eldridge: Well, we should.

Tony Carty: Well, we should, but it's not sufficient, is it?

John Eldridge: Why? I mean, I agree that there is this tendency to exclusivism built in to everything that we do. But I still think that it's something that has to be constantly put in question.

Elizabeth Templeton: Well, I think it can be put in question. I also think that because, from my theological point of view, we are not capable of our own perfection, it appears that there's going to be constant tension between vision and aspiration towards even the best kind of human inter-relating and our capacity to manage it. I think people are not innately demonic or anything, but I do think that we have tendencies which we certainly haven't yet learned to defy, if we ever will, towards self-interested resistance to other people's well-being. For example, I think there are good needs to belong, which are creative and healthful for us, but I think there are also belongings which can become very tight and hostile to others. Even family belonging can be excluding and hostile although at its best it's not. But it's tricky to keep a balance between the belonging that's necessary for good growth and the destructive narrowing kind. Family belonging isn't an absolute.

Tony Carty: Would belonging be as transient for peoples? We know families are births, marriages and deaths, individuals come and go, families fall apart, but peoples live on for generations if not for centuries

Elizabeth Templeton: Societies are transient too. But there's still enough of an illusion during a lifetime for there to be a tendency to say, 'Well, I know who I am if you describe me in this unit', whether it's family, nation or whatever. I think the surprisingness of human interaction is that this kind of unit can sometimes be transcended. We're going to have to move into a world where we more constantly transcend it in political terms, because of the connections there are in the world now, because of communication, because of economic interaction, because of the fact that what happens in one point of the globe affects the whole eco-system, for example.

John Eldridge: So, this comes back to the question of what can it mean to be interdependent in the world of nations? Does it mean that we can establish new forms of social regulation that are relatively free of military control? Can we do that? For me, one of the tragedies of the Gulf War was that in the UN, which was designed for peace, the view was that we have to have military intervention in order to liberate a small country. The problem with that, for me, ultimately was that we weren't able to think about future forms of social regulation of the international scene in ways which created new kinds of interdependence that were non-militaristic. It seems to me that we had almost within our grasp new notions of sanctions and notions of diplomacy, new ways of regulating nations whereby peace could be established. The international community really was quite out of order . We resorted once more to a military option. So I come back to the question: if we take seriously the notion of interdependence then we must ask ourselves what does that mean in practice? It cannot literally mean that power relations are abolished because there are big nations and small nations, nations with different resources. Say Ian is correct, then are powers dependent upon the fact that they have nuclear weapons because they need them or because they give a kind of symbolic power that perhaps enables them to do things that they couldn't otherwise have done? Can we move to a situation where we can operate an international community without those kinds of symbols?

Elizabeth Templeton: In a way it seems to me it is like a kind of scale model of what went on in British schools with the debate about corporal punishment. Before abolition happened everyone said it would be impossible, discipline would disappear, there would be mayhem in every classroom in the land. The fact that other countries said that they had done perfectly well without this really seemed unbelievable to people. But it has happened, and we may regret it, but ...

Tony Carty: Is there mayhem in schools? This comes back to what I mean by independence by maintaining an authentic sense of national authority, for instance. A country that has a tradition of maintaining order in schools by beating up a lot of kids then abolishing this tradition simply because it is not practised in other countries is not necessarily very clever. One has to accommodate national identities reciprocally. This is

	1960 $	1986 $	1987 $	1988 $	1990 (prov)
Global military spending	413 bn	916bn	926 bn	923 bn	880 bn
Global education spending	235 bn	878bn	903bn	928 bn	n/a
Global health spending	143 bn	759bn	794 bn	824bn	n/a

Comparisons between world military and social expenditure (all figures are at 1987 dollar prices, bn = a thousand million)

[Ruth Leger Sivard, *World Military and Social Expenditures*, 1991]

way off subject, perhaps, but a friend of mine who is a secretary in a school pointed out to me a series of articles in the *Times Educational Supplement* about mayhem in schools. Many teachers have just given up teaching and left the profession because they just couldn't cope.

Elizabeth Templeton: But it isn't entirely off track because I think if you did an analysis of what mayhem there is you would find that it's not simply the absence of the belt that's causing the mayhem but all kinds of failures to engage in constructive educational policies that would constitute preventative measures.

Tony Carty: I'm not arguing against that at all, I'm merely saying that the process of adjustment should not be mechanical but reflective and mature. I think that there's a tendency for the British to regard the Soviet Union as disintegrating because there's a conflict between the Soviet leaders which, of course, has never happened before. That is open debate in governing parties. Yet if you were to introduce that kind of pluralist democracy in Britain there would be a very loud panic and concern for a restoration of authority. So this means that we have to move from A to B rather than from A to X.

Elizabeth Templeton: Yes, but it's also David's point that it's a shift in mentality, again, from simply talking about the spurious sense of peace-keeping that this deterrent is supposed to produce to a kind of active sense of what we are doing as a people to *make* peace. To create the conditions for co-existence in which deterrent or aggressive strategy becomes both unnecessary and impossible.

Tony Carty: That's very, very complex. It's part of this colonial mentality that you build up a kind of sub-consul in a region to keep order on your behalf, for example, Israel, Iran and Iraq on the part of the US.

Elizabeth Templeton: What would it mean, for example, if the rich countries of the world cancelled the debt of the Third World? I think that would make a contribution to world peace in seconds, but it's not, by many people, related to the military situation as a real, constructive thing to do. I'm not Utopian, I don't think that you'd abolish the world's problems by any single strategy, but I think that that one would make a hell of a difference.

Ian Kellas: Can I come back to what you do about Trident? Given that we all want to move into this more hopeful kind of future, I suppose one argument for keeping it is that it makes us feel safe and we can then cope with bigger conventional arms cuts. Which is, as I understand it, why we went in for nuclear capability in the first place. We realised that we simply couldn't afford to keep a big enough army to defend ourselves. Nuclear weapons have been a cheap option. A powerful argument for not giving up Trident now is we've already paid for it.

Malcolm Spaven: Yes, and I think that's also important from the point of view of Trident as a symbol of national identity. It presents an image of strength for a state that isn't nearly as strong as that, in real terms. It seems to me that we can't simply say that we think it's awful and we'll stop it tomorrow because no state in that kind of condition is going to give up what may be its last vestiges of power or status. It has to be weaned off them in some way. Had the Trident decision not been taken, then the option was available to let the whole debate about British nuclear weapons gently fade away, and over on the Clyde there would be these four submarines just gradually falling apart and collapsing in the water. I suppose some people might not be too keen on that idea, but the thing would have just happened by default. The British state would have been quite happy with that because the last thing it would have wanted would be everybody pointing and tearing their hair out and saying, 'Oh my God, we're insecure, we're going to be attacked tomorrow because these things are falling apart'.

That option is perhaps now gone but maybe there are options for capitalising on the fact that there isn't currently a debate about Trident.

Elizabeth Templeton: Could you say more about the weaning process then? I think

I had only understood this as a kind of pressure group to decommission the thing or to—

Malcolm Spaven: Well, I've always thought that the really peculiar thing about the policy right from the start is this notion that it's no deterrent if it's not there 100% of the time. I have always thought that was a peculiar notion even when the threat was at its height, and it seems to me that now the Soviet threat has collapsed, it's plainly ridiculous. In the NATO summit in July 1990 they did discuss measures of reducing the combat readiness of particular units. Now of course, they are not going to tell anybody what those units are or what the measures were that they agreed on, but they did agree that in a situation where there is less threat then people can relax a bit and you don't have to be geared up for war as if the whole world was going to be in conflagration the day after tomorrow or even the minute after next. So maybe we can move to a situation where these submarines don't go out on patrol all the time. They only go out in particular periods or they go out to do particular exercises. It could even be argued that because of manpower shortages we can no longer afford to have two crews per submarine so we will only have one crew per submarine which means it only goes out half the time. The reasons for decisions of that sort might have to be presented differently from the real reasons and I suppose I am thinking here of a government other than the present one.

Elizabeth Templeton: But you are still thinking that it would be probable and maybe even the only realistic thing to aim for, that these new Tridents be chuntering on for the next forty years but less constantly than is currently being talked about?

Malcolm Spaven: Well, something along those lines. But then if you take that in conjunction with the Labour Party's position, for example, I think when it comes down to it, it shows that the entire edifice is fundamentally irrational. All the debates about Trident are pretty irrational in any case and so the Labour Party's position is neither here nor there. It says it will keep Trident but enter it into negotiations. The criticism of this is that if you have already stated at the beginning that you are prepared to negotiate away all your nuclear weapons, then nobody is going to listen to you anyway and you won't get any concessions from the other side. This is the school of thought that believes the way to achieve negotiations is from a position of strength and total intransigence which will force the other side to make concessions before you do.

Tony Carty: I think that comes back to the individualism, autonomism, model of Anglo-American society based on competition, mistrust and struggle, with an absence of social solidarity. I prefer Elizabeth's model of an interpersonal mutuality—identity in relation. I just do not understand why the other side is not going to negotiate with you simply because you say you are willing to negotiate openly with them—I don't understand that kind of mentality. But it is very common, for instance, in academic-government relations. If you don't kick up a big fuss and 'play hardball' the 'other side' will not take you seriously.

David Pullinger: It is true, in fact, that the ending of the Cold War came about from the opposite practice. Gorbachev said, 'We can't afford to keep developing these things. For the welfare of the USSR we need to reduce. Will you negotiate with us?' And he was quite up-front about that in his speeches. And America said 'Yes'. Not from a position of strength did Gorbachev argue in that case, but from a position of weakness and necessity.

Malcolm Spaven: Yes, but of course the American response to that would be to say, 'Well that's because we've been spending so much on the military over the last few decades, we have forced the Soviets to spend likewise which has denuded their economy of all the necessary resources and that's why they have got themselves into this crisis and are forced to negotiate'.

Tony Carty: Yes, the Americans want to say that they are right as well, but they did negotiate. Besides, another American view, Nye of Harvard, is that Soviet decline is attributable to failure to accommodate to the new information revolution. Nye thinks Reagan's arms race was an irrelevant waste of money.

John Eldridge: Yes, I think we are in unknown terrain here because there were those who argued that the way to deal with this problem was to bankrupt the Soviet Union and in a sense that is pretty much what we did. On the other hand, that was a very high risk strategy for all sorts of reasons because the Soviet Union could have chosen to have carried on. After all, it had carried on for quite a long time and could have carried on along the same lines for some time yet. All the time we were getting a more unstable situation in terms of the way the weapons were building up. But it was Gorbachev coming in who broke the way in which negotiations hitherto had carried on, which was a sort of ratchet where arms control was always moving upwards through the modernisation process. What he did was change the terms under which negotiations were held and, incidentally, made it in some ways very difficult for the Americans and for the British because we are so dependent in our economies on arms manufacturing. This we are now experiencing as an economic problem. This is a very difficult area to get a leverage on, but we now have real opportunities to restructure the way in which we organise international relations.

Ian Kellas: Well, what's the opportunity? What will we propose, because Malcolm seems to be saying 'leave them to rot' basically.

Malcolm Spaven: I hesitate to put it forward as something that we ought to be aiming for, but I think there is an argument that if Trident is basically a kind of state virility symbol, then the response of the state to people jumping up and down and saying 'Cancel Trident tomorrow' will be an even greater resolve and determination to push the thing through, and I think that this is something which is characteristic of the British state. If there are things that it believes in strongly, then it feels that it has to demonstrate, sacrifice, it has to show that it is imposing unacceptable things on society and riding through the criticism in order to achieve its aims. I think the Cruise missile debate showed that very clearly. The other matter, which I am quite closely involved with, is the whole debate about low-flying aircraft. The greater the criticism, the more the Ministry of Defence is determined to do more of it, to give more of an impression of being ready to go to war tomorrow and preparing to ride criticism and take the punishment of the politicians shouting about it and so on.

Elizabeth Templeton: But I wonder, do you really think that it's impossible to hope that the groundswell of political opinion, meaning not just the professional politicians, but people, could get to such a critical point that we couldn't stop this happening? That's really a question about democracy in the end.

Malcolm Spaven: I think it's very finely balanced. There is a point at which those paths diverge and where it is finely balanced which way you go, whether ultimately the state 'wins'. It may be a better option to try not to challenge things, not to create a debate about it which might increase the state's resolve and then you are accepting what is inevitable anyway because you realise that public opinion is just not sufficiently strong to move it.

Elizabeth Templeton: Well, I think that would be right at the moment. What you say here makes me very frightened, because the compromise with the status quo of current political opinion and government policy is just going to be, for one thing, so criminally expensive. But even if nothing ever goes wrong, even if the missiles don't get misused or blow up or cause some kind of ecological disaster, just that we will go on committing ourselves for four decades to all that is involved in maintenance and servicing, I can hardly credit as tolerable.

Tony Carty: I would agree. I think that Malcolm's analysis of the English/British political system is accurate: that is precisely what would happen if there was an attempt to remove it, but that's because this system is so committed to continuity and to an underlying tradition of military toughness, although to be fair to Major, he seems a more complex person than Heseltine or King. I am struck by a reference which some people might find obscene. When I was in Germany in the 1970s and I was in an institute which was considering the necessity for radical restructuring, one old nationalist at the table said, 'Well, you know in 1945 I was good for nothing but launching torpedoes and in 1946 I had to find something else to do'. And this business of making radical painful adjustment is something that I find in discussion with Germans. They have to face much more than we British. When I say it's rather drastic the way East Germany has to be restructured at the moment with a massive loss of employment, Germany responds, 'Well, what alternative is there if you are going to introduce an efficient and competent economic system? You can't simply go on paying to maintain salaries in the East equal to the West to maintain unproductive industrial structures'. Barnett's argument in *The Audit of War* is that it is precisely the failure to adjust which has ruined Britain. The crucial point with Trident then is how to 'weed' a political culture when it has, generally, no experience of changing its ways.

The second discrete point is that Professor Daschitschev argued in favour of the development of an international standard with respect to defence forces: they should aim to achieve the lowest level of purely defensive capacity possible, thereby accepting that, given human nature and the essentially anarchic nature of international relations, some kind of defensive capacity is necessary but it should be the lowest level possible and it should be of a particularly defensive character. Defence strategists in Germany, and I am sure every other country, have been working on the idea that there is a distinction between defensive and offensive weaponry: Trident is offensive in its nature. This, of course, leads into the problem of Star Wars, but I think what the Soviet professor was concerned to try and replace was the notion of the balance of power of which a balance of terror is a central aspect. But I think that maybe the British public wouldn't be so resistant to the idea of international elaboration of standards of minimally acceptable defensive capacity. This might be a roundabout way of tackling my first point, that is, attachment to a military, political culture.

John Eldridge: Yes. I want to come back to that, in terms of the notion of Trident as a virility symbol and so on. Allied with that is the notion that you can't challenge that because it will make the state more resistant to doing anything about it. Well, it seems to me that one of the things you do is ridicule the claim. It is clear that there are issues around the production of this missile, the production standards, issues of quality control, issues of what has happened when they have been tested and so on. In other words, you can't really claim that much for a symbol in terms of its virility if, actually, it is not all that impressive, and it seems to me that the element of ridicule is important. The second point concerns the British state. Now, I have been slightly diffident about this because I think that is too homogeneous a concept. We have been talking about pluralism. Well, the British state is also pluralist in its component parts. Yet we know perfectly well what we are thinking of, I suspect: the sort of establishment drift which has gone across the postwar period, across the parties in relation to defence policy and nuclear weapons. But what I want to argue is that the British state is itself composed of a whole lot of pluralist elements and there is space there where things can be contested, including our defence policy, and it seems to me that from that point of view there is enough rationality around to be able to challenge the basis of policy and to argue that it should be changed. After all, that happens in other situations. For example in 1945 the British state transformed itself by a whole series of policies on nationalisation which were totally at variance with all that went before. And in the 1980s, there was a complete switch around on that again—we went into privatisation. In other words, what passes for continuity in the British state should not be taken for granted.

Elizabeth Templeton: I think, also, I'd like to do more exploratory work about where are the voices, the stances, the perspectives, that need to be enabled in order to make this kind of fluidity possible. Friends in New Zealand were saying that what's been remarkable in New Zealand politics in the last decade, has been the combination of the consciousness which has come through the feminist movement and which is very much deeper and wider than it is here, and the kind of consciousness that has come through the Maori land-rights question and which infused the peace movement. The goals, the anti-virility symbol stuff plus the sense of injustice that had to be tackled by the whole society, were all pointing in an anti-militarist, anti-nuclear direction. That was what disintegrated the tendency to be able to hold on to militarism as a desirable option. Now I find that very interesting, because I know you can't engineer such shifts in social consciousness but I think you could maybe identify them and then start talking about how you enable them in terms of things like educational policy, for example.

Malcolm Spaven: I think there are a lot of interesting things there. I agree with you, John, that there is an on-going debate about safety: it's about whether the fissile material is available; there's the reactor problems. These are the kinds of things that shape the debate. How do you move on from that? How do you make that gel to such an extent that it constitutes an actual political force? It gets the message over to the wider public that perhaps it is not worth having this thing at all, maybe it's a complete waste of money and it is so unsafe that we really ought to scrap it. The problem is that that sort of debate happens about any major defence expenditure. Anything in this country that is costing £10 billion of tax-payer's money is bound to attract a certain amount of public interest, particularly if it is something highly technological. There is going to be a period of years when it's being tested, being developed and so on, when there are going to be failures—no system is perfect. There are bound to be engineering failures and so on, and the problem is that if you look at it, for example, from the point of view of parliamentary committees, they look into Trident and say, 'This is not working and that's costing rather much,' and the Ministry of Defence says, 'Well, that's rather interesting. Perhaps we ought to adjust our policy here a little bit and that's a better way; we can save some money there, and this is a better engineering solution here', and they end up with a better system. That's what democracy is supposed to be able to do for defence spending. What I am questioning is how do you turn that into something that is rather more critical and that can actually switch it over into a debate about the necessity of having the thing at all? I think it is a peculiar aspect of the debate in Britain that it seems to be very difficult to confront these things directly; we have to do it sideways through all these indirect debates about safety and value for money.

Elizabeth Templeton: But isn't that partly because there is also in Britain a real problem about effective disenfranchisement? Part of the problem is that really vast numbers of people of black or coloured ethnic minorities, or of the young, are now not thinking it worth voting at all partly because the poll tax took scores off the register at a blow. Even my most radical friends say it's not worth voting, and that the only thing you can do is go into single-issue politics and campaign through Greenpeace or through Anti-Apartheid or whatever, for this or that to change. Now that seems to me to transform us from a society which is formally democratic to one which is effectively vulnerable to the most awful kind of élitisms and fascisms and totalitarianisms, and somehow that seems to me to be the bigger, the more general political question: whether or not we can recover from people a sense that they own the politics of the country.

Tony Carty: But you say recover. When have they owned the politics of the country?

John Eldridge: In 1945 when people came back from the war and actually wanted to see a different kind of society. We can speak about all the things that happened after that and things didn't work out as everybody hoped, nevertheless people did come back with new hopes, with new aspirations—and structures were changed. To me this is very important. It meant that there were new powers of ownership, new forms of administration. Some of them were experimental and some of them didn't work, but they were real genuine transformations.

Elizabeth Templeton: Or in the 1830s, 1840s, 1850s.

Tony Carty: It's very difficult, I suppose, to be specific about this. I simply feel foreign relations have always been a private matter for Her Majesty and her advisers at the time you are talking about. I take your point and I don't want to play it down, but you have a few people deciding if Britain should have a nuclear squib, and that laager mentality that the defence establishment has is the sort of thing Malcolm is talking about, that they would feel they had to carry on in the face of misunderstanding and mistrust on the part of foolish people who really don't know how things function. These 'foolish' people often do appear to be very foolish—they are certainly very self-righteous and it's very difficult to know what to think. That's why I am inclined to the view that we should try to keep on internationalising the debate, to draw British political culture out of itself. For instance, one concrete proposal was the Soviet one: that we worked towards international standards of minimum levels of effective defensive capacity, completely side-stepping the pacifist argument that not only are we not threatened, but we never have been, which I don't think is true. Certainly it is not the Soviet view. For instance, Professor Daschitschev argues that the Soviet Union, up until 1987, certainly tried to constitute a threat. I was once caught up quite short at a meeting in Moscow by a Ukranian academic who said, 'This country has done an awful lot which was quite inexcusable'. So that's one level. Another point I would make to Malcolm, and it's just one of these egghead ideas, is, haven't the Soviets at some point made an offer to pool defence research and strategy? Why not undertake to continue the development of this idiotic Trident system but in collaboration with the Soviets and see whether they have got any ideas about how to improve the system—then sell it to the Japanese? At least at that rate we could recover some economic benefit.

Elizabeth Templeton: I agree with you about the laager mentality, but I think there is also a risk of demonising them. I remember hearing an account by Helen Steven of discussions on Iona where she invited twenty-five of the top military bods and began by saying to them, 'Now, we are here because we are all concerned about how to maintain peace'. She didn't set off to polarise them with the kind of view, 'You wicked people—here I am as a pacifist to tell you the right way to do it'. She worked through forty-eight hours of trying to establish what was common ground and shared vision and why it diverged at different points. Now I think again this is a peace-making issue. It's people with the kind of imagination to find touchable nerves in those who currently control policy, but also to enable those who could have more of a grip on it, if they were willing, to accept it, and these seem to me to be simultaneous needs.

Malcolm Spaven: Well, I don't know if you are familiar with the work of the Oxford Research Group: it was set up in about 1983, more or less with the sort of aims that you have just been talking about, to try and approach people, specifically individuals who had some key role in the nuclear weapons decision-making process, initially in Britain but also they started looking at other countries too. The idea was to engage these people in debate, or rather discussion, with groups of ordinary concerned citizens. They would be contacted by letter and the group would try to set up meetings with decision-makers, or at least continue the exchange of letters and do it very much on a person-to-person basis and not let it become the person's parliamentary secretary or some official who would answer the letter. But eventually it became more the case that the people who actually worked in the Oxford Research Group, as opposed to the groups of citizens, ended up speaking directly to key individuals, going to dinner with them, going to meetings where there were lots of other academics present, and I think the project was rather diverted into just being part of the military establishment's discussions with, essentially, itself. So I agree with the principle: I think the principle is wonderful and I think that

Helen Steven's experience in Iona was terrific. But what I would question is, how far does that go beyond the individuals who are directly involved in the experience? Because it has to get translated from a feeling of personal satisfaction, maybe even a certain amount of changing of minds personally, that has to get translated into changes in the institutional structure.

Elizabeth Templeton: I am sure that's right and I think it's one of these drop-in-the-bucket kind of things at any point where you start it. But I think for me that politicians of almost all parties have lost answerability because they are no longer trusting their electorate as conversation partners. They are sloganising over their heads and I think that the kind of political malaise of the country will not be healable unless different groups on all kinds of issues start doing this.

Ian Kellas: I think this idea that we have been disenfranchised is a red herring because I don't really believe that people were ever properly represented in the past. My feeling is that Britain's problem is basically success. It's been an outrageously successful political force. It's had the biggest empire in history. It's got rid of it efficiently. It's this tiny little island with a bloody awful climate and modest natural resources but it discovered a particular political and economic system, with the factory as the essential element, way before anybody else did. And the problem is now that our political apparatus is out of date. It is based on the adversarial system which has been mirrored in the recent international stalemate—there are the goodies and there are the baddies—and this whole thing cuts right through our society, our thinking and political system, right down the middle of the House of Commons. There are the goodies on one side and the baddies on the other and you can only vote for the goodies or the baddies. And now we are entering into a world which is obviously plural and we have to find ways to come to terms with this.

Tony Carty: This is the club mentality as well, the club is part of the game. You are talking about the adversarial scene—the scene of the game is the contest; and, at the end of the day, there is really nothing at stake except the game itself.

David Pullinger: I think this is where we vary with fundamentalists, of course. This is why I think they have such trouble looking at diplomacy with Islamic fundamentalism. They believe in what they are doing, whereas I think that the game is the game within British society.

Tony Carty: You see, you have to give people another game to play.

John Eldridge: It's also a deadly game that we are talking about—defence and nuclear weapons. While you are right about the fact that there's this adversarial business built in, one of the criticisms that was made by the Thatcher administration was that we had reached some sort of consensus across the parties. Yet that consensus certainly included a defence policy, and people who were outside that consensus were usually labelled either as starry-eyed idealists or as in the pay of the Kremlin. So there was that sort of consensus that, as it were, undergirded this adversarial system and I think that's what we have to contend with. How can we find a voice in discussions that says to that consensus, 'Look, there are other ways of viewing this and there are other kinds of assumptions that we can make. And please don't label us starry-eyed idealists when actually we may be more pragmatic than you are, or more realistic than you are in terms of the survival of the world, and please don't tell us we are in the pay of the Kremlin because that is old hat anyway'?

Elizabeth Templeton: But I think I'm not so willing to be convinced or not so convinced, or a bit of both, that the political history of Britain should be read with such cynicism. I think I

Extracts from Official Secrets Acts

Official Secrets Act 1911, Section 1:

This section of the Act was designed to deal with foreign espionage, but its terms are extremely wide ranging. It outlaws the acquisition 'for any purpose prejudicial to the safety or interests of the State' of information 'which is calculated to be or might be or is intended to be directly or indirectly useful to an enemy'. It is possible to be prosecuted under this section of the Act if one 'approaches, inspects, passes over or is in the neighbourhood of, or enters any prohibited place within the meaning of this Act'.

Further, under subsection 1.(2) of the Act, it is not even necessary for the Crown to prove any particular guilty act; an accused person can be convicted 'if, from the circumstances of the case, or his conduct, or his known character as proved, it appears that his purpose was a purpose prejudicial to the safety or interests of the State'.

Nowhere in the original 1911 Act is the term 'the safety or interests of the State' defined.

Section 2 of the original 1911 Official Secrets Act was designed to prevent unauthorised disclosure by government employees of information 'which relates to or is used in a prohibited place or anything in such a place'.

However, following government embarrassment over a number of attempts to prosecute civil servants under this section of the Act during the 1980s, and growing concern about publication of revealing books by former members of the security and intelligence services—most notably Peter Wright's *Spycatcher*—Section 2 (but not the other sections) was repealed by a new Official Secrets Act in 1989.

The 1989 Act was designed to restrict the wide remit of the original Section 2, replacing it with a more specifically worded Act which protected more limited classes of official information.

In respect of defence information, unauthorised disclosure under the 1989 Act is only an offence if it is 'damaging' to either the capability of the armed forces, or to Britain's interests abroad. But the Act's definition of defence information whose disclosure would be damaging is wide, encompassing, for example, defence policy as well as technical details of weaponry and forces.

read the nineteenth century's battles for suffrage, for example, as expressing a real commitment in the bulk of people that they felt they got some kind of grip on their destiny and that the party system as it emerged was less important than this sense that whichever of the parties it was, it had to be answerable to more and more people, and the virtue of nineteenth century Britain was that it was going in that direction. I find the adversarial thing now nonsense, which is quite cynically exploited by those who are in positions of power, but I think we have lost control relative to what the situation was pre-war and maybe recently post-war, in terms of political information, political confidence, political—

Tony Carty: I think this is all true but I think that the question is, in our context, to bring it back into the focus of Trident. There are many different ways to try to do that. I would think that you are talking about political decay and I think the notion of Trident, the notion of having a squib as a form of virility, as a status symbol of our power, is also a form of decay. I think that what has happened historically is that Britain has been an aristocratic oligarchy and in the course of the nineteenth century and in parts of the twentieth century, there has been a massive liberal populist attempt to break through. But I don't think this push has ever reached the point of establishing a kind of modern democracy in the sense that you have on the Continent. Consider the foreign relations powers of the government, Her Majesty's prerogative in respect of foreign affairs, the secret service and official secrets, the general notion of the state's affairs being private. Consider the terms of the 1989 Official Secrets Act and foreign affairs questioning. I feel very much like your radical friends that the Labour Party appals me every bit as much as the Conservative Party in terms of its structures and its ambitions. So where does one go forward?

Official Secrets Acts (cont'd)

The Act introduces a new defence: if an accused can show that they did not know the disclosed material related to defence, security or intelligence, or did not know that it might be damaging, then they can plead ignorance. But there has been widespread criticism that the new Act does not enshrine in law a 'public interest defence': a civil servant cannot argue that he/she disclosed the information because he/she felt that it served a wider public interest which went beyond the requirements for secrecy. Although this had not been established in the original Acts either, the cases of civil servants Sarah Tisdall and Clive Ponting in the 1980s had created a significant public debate about the ability of civil servants to follow their consciences.

Britain is increasingly isolated among democratic nations in preferring to legislate for official secrecy rather than for freedom of information. Laws providing for varying degrees of government openness and freedom of information exist in France, the Netherlands, the Scandinavian countries, the USA, Canada, New Zealand and Australia.

David Pullinger: Can I add that we haven't changed our view in the use of technological tools. We are the only nation still that will not allow somebody to use a tool for their job unless their manager has also got that tool—even though they may not need it for their job. This comes in computing, it comes in all sorts of things, and it is a major problem in management in Britain. And so when we are talking about tools, war and symbols, this penetrates right the way through society. I have worked on research projects where we have not been able to introduce new technology because it is argued that, if we introduce tools for these people to do this particular research project, everyone would have to have one and then all their managers would have to have one, and that they couldn't afford to do it. The civil service took that view. The MoD argued the same to us. And so did one university. I think this shows the view of tools as status symbols penetrates right the way through all sections of our society.

Malcolm Spaven: This is akin in some ways to the baroque arsenal arguments. I have been through two universities in the last five years that were in the process of introducing new telephone systems, both at the cost of roughly £1 million. The problem was the telephone systems that are available on the market—partly because they come from industries that have been very dependent on military work in the past—are over-blown. The technology is too far advanced. They do all kinds of things—you press a few buttons and you can have conference calls etc, which most people don't actually need. You could have a far simpler telephone system, far cheaper, which would cause far less disruption to the organisation to introduce. We haven't tailored the technology sufficiently to our organisation.

Can I come back on disenfranchisement? You mentioned in 1945 there was a real feeling that the state was somehow in the people's hands, that we had been through the experiences of the war and that there had been new state structures set up which were more geared to planning society, and doing that in a democratic way and on a national basis. We are now in a situation where many of the institutions that were set up then are being, or have been, dismantled. At the same time there has been a collapse of most of the big national—and nationalised—industries and there has been a move away from mass industrial employment. So people's allegiances have switched from a national level and switched also away from the state towards private enterprise. People's allegiances are different, but I think many people still have a need in Britain to identify with, perhaps, a more overarching institution, something that represents Britain. They want to be able to feel British, and the only thing that's left is this rump of the state which is basically the military. And it's partly because, as you said, Tony, foreign affairs have traditionally been separated off from the democratic pressures that some of the other elements of the state have been subjected to. That has enabled the military core of the state to persist. So you could almost argue that Trident represents the lost politics that you speak of. What I wonder is, given that we now have a more decentralised and pluralist economy, compared to twenty, thirty, forty years ago, are we perhaps now in the situation where we need to rebuild political institutions at a lower level which can start to rebuild those lost politics? Although I have never been terribly convinced of arguments for devolution, maybe this is an argument for it. Perhaps the creation of a Scottish assembly, and maybe regional assemblies in other parts of Britain, would help to pull people back into politics, remind them that they have a right to talk about things and to debate things which, currently, they just accept as given; and maybe that will ultimately rekindle political debate nationally too.

John Eldridge: Well, I think we are reaching the end of our time and if I was chairman I would come up with some very eloquent summary! I think that we have had a very full discussion. I am sure that there are things that all of us wish we had said, even though we have been going for several hours. But it's time to draw to a close. Thank you.

Afterword

T*he conviction of all the contributors to this book is that the present, with all its fears, uncertainties and prophecies of doom, is a time of opportunity to think imaginatively about the future.*

(Davis, *Ethics and Defence*, p 270)

What applied then, applies now. We hope that the give-and-take format of this conversation will be a kind of invitation to participate in a larger open debate about how our society understands itself at present. For we share a sense, strengthening the more we register the Trident data, that it is the symbolic, almost 'mythical' importance of Trident which really lies behind its commissioning rather than any specific strategic or tactical role for it on the current world scene.

Particularly as we embark on the newly emerging post-Cold War Europe, we consider it vital that we appreciate the perspective that other Europeans have of us. For they may see, more clearly than we do, how our supposed 'independence' on the nuclear front is in fact tightly bound up with US policy and economic decisions. Indeed, the whole credibility gap between the US/British account of the US as the great white liberator of the oppressed, and the widespread global sense of the damaging impact of so much US policy on other parts of the world, might provide a salutary jolt to any complacency about our military allegiances.

In the appraisal of Trident, not only have we tried to address the immediate questions about its relevance or irrelevance in any military scenario, but also to get behind them to a range of even bigger questions. How much are the policy decisions of governments determined by economic needs, so that the debate about Trident can only be realistic when placed in the context of Britain's involvement in the military-industrial complex? How far is any government answerable to its electorate on such issues? Is 'democracy' a cynically exploited mask for policies which are focused almost with their own self-propagating momentum, whatever the formal political structure? Have we reached a point in world history where the interconnectedness of one bit of the world with another means the bankruptcy of old models of individual nationalism? If so, how do we create for people a vivid and satisfying alternative to the isolationist, excluding forms of national myth which carry so much of the military razzmatazz in their wake? How do we create an internationalism which is not abstract and alienating and bureaucratic, but earthed in communication and cherishing of distinctive identities?

The microcosmic upheavals of Europe at present, in Yugoslavia, in the Baltic States, in the new Germany, make these real issues with which we all need to be grappling. They will not be issues resolved by slick dogma, but with collaborative and sensitive exploration.

In this context particularly, let alone the larger global one of environmental threat, pandemic famine and desperate poverty, Trident seems to us a relic of a mentality which can no longer be creative, and yet which will consume billions of pounds worth of money in maintenance and servicing beyond the billions already spent on its construction. Though some in the group are pacifist, not all are; and our complaint against *this* weapon system does not depend on a utopian view of the world in which we envisage the abolition of war. *This* programme, offered in official propaganda as the brightest and best development Britain could hope for, seems to us clearly discredited as relevant of worthwhile resources for any conceivable military or political purpose. To demythologise the rhetoric of that propaganda is, we hope, a contribution worth making.

I want to place the discussion into a theological context with the suggestion that one core direction of the Christian doctrine of God is that we move from any concept of 'security' which depends on images of impregnable resistance to invasion, to one which presupposes a horizon of collaboration in which all creation has to be involved. Only if we can generate imaginative responsiveness to the sense that we happily depend on one another in mutuality for the sustaining of any future, can we hope to reverse the competitive destructiveness of many of our existing modes of 'making ourselves secure'.

This obviously is easier said than done, but it should be clear that this can be no bland and self-evident agenda, even in terms of global prudence. To live with an open, inclusive view of security is, in some ways, to live 'against the grain'. For, whatever is true of the inner life of God, it is immediate and palpable that we are quite vulnerable beings, and threaten one another. A finite natural environment assaults us with ageing, illness, accident and untimely death. In that context, we instinctively compete for land, property, employment, and even for the less concrete goals of esteem, reputation and moral superiority. We have modes of self-identification which root us deeply in natural and cultural groups, boundaried by family, sex, creed, nationality, language and so on.

The religious 'core' of this conversation is not the standard 'pacifist' versus 'non-pacifist' reading of Scripture or Church traditions. Rather, it lies around the question of how we see our identity and our relationships with other nations. This can, of course, be answered quite non-religiously. But we are, perhaps, suggesting that the potency of myths about Britain and its military virility, for instance, are best explained as quasi-religious: deeply felt images of identity whose loss threatens our corporate sense of safety. To be opening up such questions of where we find identity and safety as a people is moving deeper than the normal pragmatic concerns of day-to-day politics.

As we consider 'security', we should take quite seriously the images of human community which Christianity suggests as the condition of what is sometimes called 'The Kingdom of God'; where in the likeness of God himself, some would say in participation in the very life of God, security is to do with a stability of mutual life-giving and receiving without constraint and without limit.

'Taking it seriously' does not mean that it can be turned into instant ethics or politics. But it does, I think, exert some leverage on our more complacent accounts of security which have to do with the adequate containment of our enemies, the adequate safeguarding of our present interests, the projection of our present structures into an indefinite future.

In particular, I think it invites us to see '*national*' security as an idolatrous goal if it takes precedence over the more challenging security of creation which is willing to acknowledge the vulnerability which interdependence means for us.

For Scottish people especially, the issue of identity and nationalism is currently live: and it is an irony that this 'token' of supposed British strength and security should be lodging here—though of course there are inter-related, Trident-related activities going on in many parts of Britain. We hope that the importance of responding actively to Trident's launching is clear to Scots inside and outside the Churches. And the enlargement of this small conversation, with attentiveness and candour, would be one contribution to genuine 'local democracy', whatever political structure undergirds it.

Elizabeth Templeton

Woops! Frightfully sorry Mr Gorbacher, please don't take it personally

Goodbye To All That?

One big theme in these conversations was the disintegration of the Soviet Union. Now we have witnessed, courtesy of satellite television, the short-lived coup and the dramatic events surrounding it. The Communist party itself stands discredited and the public symbols of the party rule are being dismantled. Statues of Lenin are coming down and it will be no surprise if his body is removed from the mausoleum in Red Square. The future of the Soviet Union, even as a loose confederation of states, is uncertain.

And where does this leave Trident? Targeted on Moscow it could destroy the Russian Parliament, Boris Yeltsin, Mikhail Gorbachev and millions of Moscow citizens. To state this now, in the wake of all that has happened, is to underline the absurdity of this weapon.

Whatever our judgements about the past and the role of nuclear weapons, the Cold War is over. Therein lies the challenge to Britain to re-think its foreign and defence policy. The question must be plainly asked: is Britain's commitment to an independent nuclear deterrent realistic in this changing world? Is this not now the time to break with our past and abandon these dangerous and irrelevant symbols of world status? They belonged to yesterday's world. Can our politicians measure up to the challenges and opportunities of these new times?

> Then let us pray that come it may,
> (As come it will for a' that),
> That Sense and Worth, o'er a' the earth
> Shall bear the gree[1] an' a' that.
>
> *Burns*

[1] gree = have priority

September 1991

References in Conversations

Barnett, C: *The Collapse of British Power* (Eyre Methuen 1972 and Alan Sutton 1984).

Barnett, C: *The Audit of War; the illusion & reality of Britain as a great nation* (Macmillan 1986 and Papermac 1987).

Chomsky, N: *Human Rights and American Foreign Policy*.

Davis, H (ed): *Ethics and Defence: Power and Responsibility in the Nuclear Age* (Blackwell 1986).

Fulbright, J W: *The Arrogance of Power* (Jonathon Cape 1967 and Penguin 1970).

Ishihara, S: *The Japan That Can Say No* (Simon & Schuster 1991).

Kennedy, P M: *The Rise and Fall of the Great Powers: Economic Change and Military Conflict from 1500 to 2000* (Fontana 1989).

Leigh, D: *The Wilson Plot* (Heinemann 1988).

Nye, J: *America: Bound to Lead* (1989).
    and Lectures to JFK Institute (Berlin, June 1991).

Discriminate Deterrence: Report of the Commission on Integrated Long-term Strategy (US Government Printing Office, Washington DC, January 1988)

Report of the Select Committee on Overseas Trade (House of Lords Session 1984-85), p 238-1. par 7.

Ullman: 'The Covert French Connection' in *Foreign Policy* No 75 (Summer 1989), 3-33.

See also:

McKenzie, D: *Inventing Accuracy* (MIT Press 1991).

Contributors

Tony Carty
Senior Lecturer in International Law, University of Glasgow
Professor in Law and Politics, Free University of Berlin

John Eldridge
Professor of Sociology, University of Glasgow

Ian Kellas
Cartoonist

David Pullinger
Director, SRT Project, Church of Scotland

Malcolm Spaven
Research Fellow in Sociology, University of Edinburgh

Elizabeth Templeton
Theologian and writer